Images of
ELVIS

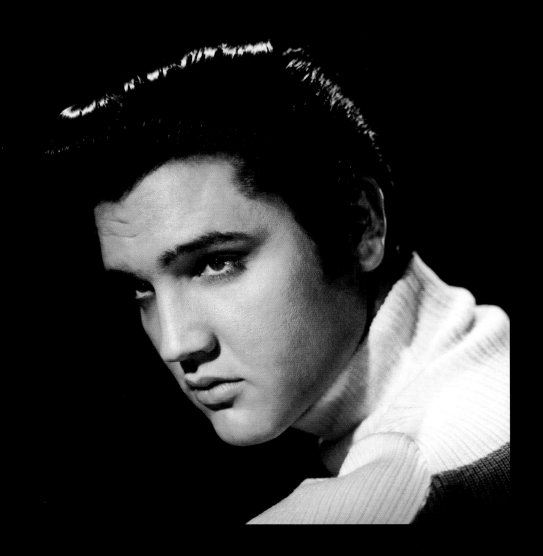

Images of
Elvis

Marie Clayton

PaRragon

Bath · New York · Singapore · Hong Kong · Cologne · Delhi · Melbourne

This edition published by Parragon in 2007

Parragon
Queen Street House
4 Queen Street
Bath, BA1 IHE

For photograph copyrights see page 224
Text © Parragon Books Ltd 2006

Produced by Atlantic Publishing

A catalogue record for this book is available
from the British Library.

ISBN 978-1-4054-8296-7
Printed in Indonesia

INTRODUCTION

There can be few entertainers who have inspired such long-lasting devotion as Elvis Presley. Years after his death, stores are still full of his records and his image is instantly recognizable around the world. He is more than just a singer who died – he is a true American folk hero. Elvis himself once said, "When I was a boy, I was the hero in comic books and movies. I grew up believing in a dream. Now, I've lived it out. That's all a man can ask for."

Elvis was born on January 8, 1935, to a family so poor that they could not afford medical care, so his older twin brother, Jesse, was stillborn. Despite their circumstances, Gladys insisted that Elvis learned good manners and show respect to his elders – a training that stayed with him for the rest of his life. She constantly impressed upon him that he was special and different from other people. He grew up rather shy and dreamy and a bit of a loner, and music became a release from the constraints of his life. As a young boy he enjoyed black R&B, jazz, and soul music, as well as gospel music and country 'n' western. His family had no money to pay for lessons so he taught himself to play the piano and learnt the guitar from family friends. He had a memory for words and music and was able to sing or play a song after hearing it once or twice. He entered his first singing competition at the age of 10 and came second, winning $5 and free admission to the fairground rides.

In Memphis the Presleys lived near Beale Street, legendary home of the blues. Elvis admired the singers' sense of style and color, and developed his own look, combining strong colors and sharp tailoring with long, slicked-back hair and sideburns. Typical outfits included a bolero jacket bought from Lanskys – a tailor on Beale Steet – and pants with a bright stripe down the side of the leg, or a bright pink suit teamed with white suede shoes. It was very different from the cropped, preppy look of most other teenagers. At first he aspired to be a gospel singer, but also played hillbilly music and soon developed his own sound, which later became known as rockabilly and then rock 'n' roll.

In 1953, Elvis – by that time working as a truck driver – turned up at Sun Studios in Memphis. With guitarist Scotty Moore and bass-player Bill Black he recorded an old blues number, "That's All Right, Mama," which Dewey Phillips – a popular and influential local DJ – played numerous times in one evening, telling listeners it was sure to be a hit. Elvis and the Blue Moon Boys began to play regularly at the Eagle's Nest in Memphis, and the *Louisiana Hayride*, broadcast on KWKH from Shreveport's Municipal Auditorium. Late in 1954, they met Colonel Tom Parker, a music promoter who had started out in carnival. With his help, Elvis moved onto a national stage and was soon headlining shows across the country. Women went crazy as he shook his hips or jiggled his legs and some religious leaders took exception to his "lewd" movements and called for him and his music to be banned.

RCA gave Elvis a contract late in 1955 and the following year released "Heartbreak Hotel." It was a phenomenal hit, going to No. 1 in the charts, and by the middle of 1956 Elvis was bringing in over 50 percent of RCA's income. In August 1956, he began work on his first movie, *Love Me Tender*, and after he appeared on *The Ed Sullivan Show* advance orders of two million were received for the title single. The movie opened in five hundred theaters that November, and was a huge hit despite poor reviews.

Elvis purchased Graceland, a colonial-style mansion, in March 1957 and lived there with various members of the "Memphis Mafia," along with a changing population of band members, backup singers, and starlets. By now he was earning a fortune and could eat whatever he wished – but he had a real weakness for junk food, particularly sliced-banana and peanut butter sandwiches, greasy doughnuts, fried or mashed potatoes and dark brown gravy. This diet was beginning to cause a weight problem – although he was still burning off many calories in nervous energy.

Elvis was inducted into the United States Army in March 1958, going to Fort Hood in Texas for basic training and then to Germany. Although he had never been abroad he was greeted by thousands of ecstatic fans when his ship docked at Bremerhaven. During his two years in the Army he was promoted twice, leaving with the rank of sergeant. He came out fifteen pounds lighter than when he went in, but was still addicted to junk food and was now also taking amphetamines. He had apparently used them to stay awake during

Opposite: Elvis's second movie, Loving You, was originally entitled Lonesome Cowboy.

night maneuvers, but now took them on a daily basis, partly to keep slim. The pills not only caused unpredictable mood swings but also contributed to Elvis's growing disconnection from the normal world.

Before he left Elvis had recorded several songs to release in his absence and a steady stream of stories about his life in the Army had kept his career alive. In May 1960 he made an appearance on a Frank Sinatra special, revealing a new, mature, laid-back style which lost a few fans but picked up many more – he was still one of the most popular singers in America. After the show, he returned to the studio to record new songs, and then to begin the soundtrack for a new movie, *GI Blues*. The storyline of *GI Blues* was very lightweight and capitalized on Elvis's time in the Army. His character was a soldier who also happened to be a musician, and who fell in love with a cabaret singer. It was set in Germany, but all Elvis's scenes were shot in Hollywood. It marked a change from his previous movies in that he was no longer playing a bad boy who makes good, but a safe and wholesome character. He also completed a western, *Flaming Star*, in 1960 and began shooting on *Wild in the Country*, both of which

allowed him to move away from his singing a little and tackle slightly more dramatic roles.

During 1961 Elvis performed live only three times – two concerts at the Ellis Auditorium in Memphis and a charity event for the USS *Arizona* at Bloch Arena at Pearl Harbor, Hawaii. The live appearances had become a danger to all concerned – Elvis had to arrive and leave in the greatest secrecy as the fans behaved so wildly in their attempts to reach him that there was a real risk that someone would soon get hurt. Elvis was also now concentrating on his movie career, and since he went on to make three pictures a year for most of the rest of the sixties there was little time left for concert tours. Almost all his movies were conceived as a vehicle for their star – lightweight stories with songs worked into the script. A typical offering was *Blue Hawaii*, a musical comedy built round an exotic location, which was a massive hit.

In Germany Elvis had been introduced to Priscilla Beaulieu, stepdaughter of an army officer, and although she was only fourteen they saw each other regularly. He had remained in touch and in March

Above: Elvis and Priscilla on their wedding day, May 1, 1967.
Opposite: Elvis records with the Jordanaires in 1956.

1962 he asked her parents if she could come to visit him. She was still only seventeen, so Elvis suggested she should finish her schooling in America. They did everything together and he began to mold her into his perfect woman. At Christmas 1966 they finally became engaged, and the wedding was set for May 1,1967, in Las Vegas. After Lisa Marie Presley was born on February 1,1968, Elvis announced he was the happiest man in the world.

However, his career was in trouble. The quality of his movies had been declining so that only the most ardent fans would pay to see them, and most of the records were selling poorly. A change of direction was clearly needed. For a TV special broadcast just before Christmas 1968, Elvis wore black leather and belted out his rock 'n' roll hits, finishing with a brand new song, "If I can Dream." It was a total triumph – hearing him sing the old hits with an exciting new freshness was a revelation. Soon afterward Elvis recorded some of his best material to date, with "In the Ghetto" giving him a major hit and a gold record. From 1969 to 1977 Elvis played a total of almost 1,100 concerts despite failing health. Although at the beginning he was obviously enjoying himself on stage, toward the end he was just going through the motions. The punishing schedule was principally for the money – Elvis had established a costly lifestyle, with large numbers of people relying on him for a living. He was also outrageously generous – not only to people he knew well but also to perfect strangers.

After Lisa Marie was born, Elvis had made it plain to Priscilla that he was no longer physically attracted to her. Unhappy and

Opposite: Elvis dressed in black leather during the "Comeback Special" and (above) in one of his trademark white jumpsuits.

unfulfilled, she began an affair and in 1971 she told her husband that she no longer loved him. In October 1973 their divorce was finalized and a few days later Elvis was admitted to hospital. Newspapers reported he had collapsed because he was so upset about the ending of his marriage, but in reality he had suffered a serious reaction to the all the prescription drugs he was taking, which had also caused his behavior to become increasingly erratic, both in private and on stage. After quietly going through a drug withdrawal program in hospital, he was nursed back to health.

When he returned to Las Vegas toward the end of January 1974, Elvis was slimmer and fitter than he had been for years. He was still taking an assortment of pills but doctors had worked out a daily program, adding multivitamins and substituting placebos for some. However, the music had become slick and lacking in excitement; Elvis sang without emotion and often stopped and addressed the audience

on any subject that took his fancy. By the end of 1974 he had regained weight and was severely depressed. He spent his 40th birthday in seclusion, and at the end of January was rushed back into hospital. Within a few months he was rapidly gaining weight again, and finding the drugs he wanted despite attempts to stop him. During concerts he often appeared exhausted – but the fans still loved him.

At the end of July, Lisa Marie came to Graceland for a two-week visit and Elvis seemed in a good mood for most of the time. On August 15 had visited the dentist and later played some racquetball, settling down to try and sleep in the early hours of the following morning. Despite three lots of medication he was unable to settle, and early in the afternoon of the 16th he was found lying on the floor of his bathroom. The King of rock 'n' roll was dead.

Images of
ELVIS

Starting out

Right: In October 1954, Elvis and the Blue Moon Boys appeared for the first time on the *Louisiana Hayride*, which was broadcast on KWKH from Shreveport's Municipal Auditorium. The *Hayride* reached twenty-eight states and was much more innovative than the Mecca of country singing, Nashville's Grand Ole Opry. Elvis and the Boys had played the Opry once, but their raw new style did not go down well – after the performance Elvis was advised to stick to driving trucks! By contrast, at the Hayride they were an instant hit and were quickly invited back and then contracted to appear every Saturday night.

Opposite: Elvis leans over the edge of the stage at the Olympia Theater, Miami, pointing at the frantic teenage girls who are trying to reach him from the orchestra pit.

Contradictions

Left: Part of Elvis's appeal was that he was a mass of contradictions: he appeared shy and polite but, onstage, moved in a way that drove women crazy; he belted out rock 'n' roll numbers but sang gospel with true feeling; he was quietly spoken and loved his mother, but was also an audacious youth who encouraged teenagers to rebel.

Opposite: Elvis belting out a song on stage. He had soon gained a huge following of fans, mainly teenage girls, who would attend whenever he was performing. He was quick to encourage the girls in the audience, teasing and swiveling his hips to drive them wild. It was not only his movements that were suggestive – the release of "Baby, Let's Play House" in April 1955 caused a major stir because of its suggestive lyrics. However, the fans loved it and it became the first of his records to go into the national charts. Just a month later, Elvis signed a management contract with Colonel Tom Parker. The Colonel had started out in carnival but moved into showbusiness after he became manager of singer Eddy Arnold.

Going for Gold!

Above: Elvis shows the gold record for "Heartbreak Hotel" to drummer D.J. Fontana, singer Gordon Stoker and guitarist Scotty Moore. The experienced Scotty – along with bass player Bill Black – had first been teamed with Elvis by Sam Phillips of Sun Studios and after weeks of rehearsing they recorded "That's All Right, Mama." Demos were quickly sent out to local radio stations and Dewey Phillips – one of the most popular and influential DJs in the area – played the record fourteen times in one evening on WHBQ, telling listeners it was sure to be a hit.

Opposite: Even before he was famous, Elvis was a snappy dresser. He had been brought up near Beale Street in Memphis, the legendary home of the Blues, and he admired the way the black singers there moved. He also liked their sense of style and color, and soon developed his own look which combined bold colors, sharp tailoring, and long, slicked-back hair. Typical outfits included a bolero jacket and pants with a bright stripe down the side of the leg, and a bright pink suit teamed with white suede shoes.

Heartbreak Hotel

Left: The Gold disk for "Heartbreak Hotel" was awarded after 500,000 copies had been sold, the Platinum when sales reached 1,000,000 copies. The single was Elvis's first release for RCA after the Colonel arranged for the label to buy his contract from Sam Phillips. Initially RCA was very disappointed that "Heartbreak Hotel" sounded so different from the previous songs he had recorded. Some of the top men at RCA even wondered if they had made a costly mistake, but the single was a huge hit, swiftly reaching No.1 in the charts. By mid-1956, Elvis was bringing in more than half of RCA's total income.

Opposite: Elvis singing and playing the piano during a recording session for RCA.

First movie contract

Left: Elvis uses the roof of a taxi cab as he signs autographs for a group of girls in Nashville in April 1956. His music appealed to a young audience who were rebelling against authority. They wanted their own music – preferably something their parents disapproved of, and rock 'n' roll fitted the bill perfectly. Elvis never saw himself as a rebel as he had grown up with the kind of music he now played. He was becoming well known across America, but the Colonel already had his eye on the next move. Early in April Elvis had a screen test and was quickly signed up to a seven-year, three-movie contract with Paramount Pictures.

The Jordanaires

Above and opposite: Elvis recording a new song in April 1956 with the Jordanaires – Gordon Stoker, Neal Matthews Jnr., Hoyt Hawkins, and Hugh Jarrett – with Bill Black on bass and D.J. Fontana on drums. Elvis first worked with the Jordanaires as his backing group in 1956 and continued to do so until 1970. They performed on all of his RCA recordings and at all of his concerts in this period, as well as either playing on the soundtrack, or appearing in, twenty-eight movies. Elvis's first love was gospel music, and the Jordanaires were originally formed as a gospel quartet, covering both black and white gospel music, so they were all on the same musical wavelength. Even when not recording, they often got together just to perform gospel for their own pleasure.

Friendship begins

Right: Although Elvis had first appeared in Las Vegas in April 1956 – at the New Frontier Hotel – it had not been a great success. The venue's middle-class audience was more used to sophisticated entertainers like Frank Sinatra, and did not take to the raw energy of Elvis's rock 'n' roll. However, in one respect the time spent there was a success, as Elvis met Liberace and the two men subsequently became great friends. Liberace advised the new star on how to dress to please his audience and also encouraged him to sort out his skin problems and to have his teeth capped.

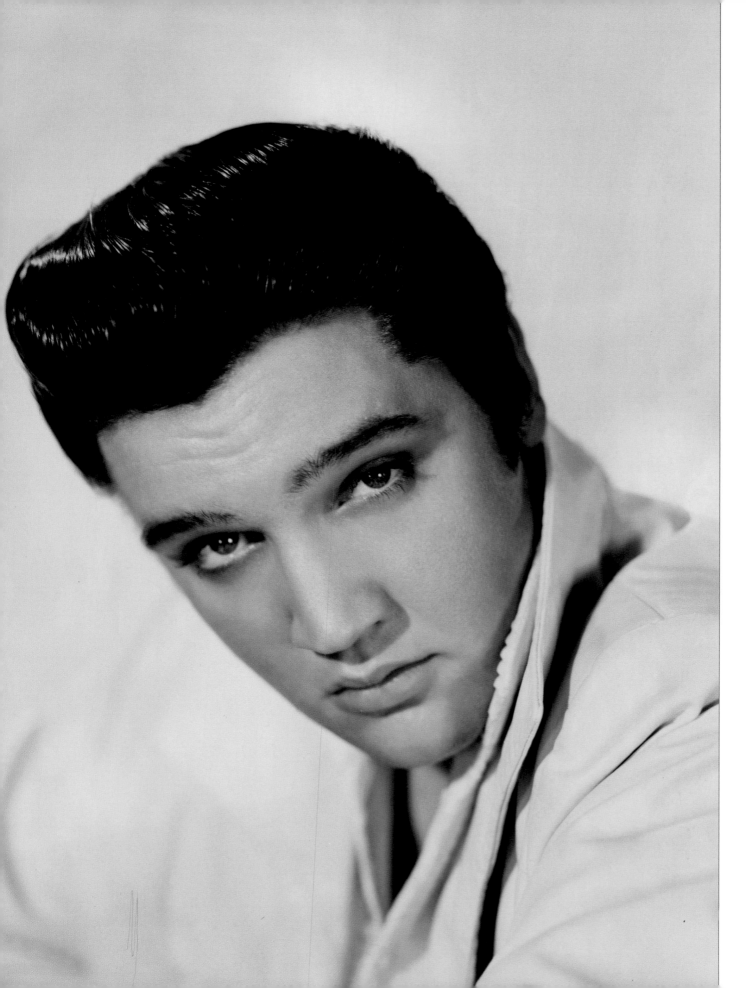

King held hostage by a Queen...

Left: A publicity shot of Elvis from the late 1950s. The Colonel's business abilities and promotional skills were already famous even before he became Elvis's manager and he soon made a big difference to his new star's career. Early in 1956 Elvis first appeared on *The Milton Berle Show* – broadcast live from the deck of the USS *Hancock*, which was docked in San Diego. The show included a comedy sketch in which Milton played Melvin Presley, the long-lost brother of Elvis.

Opposite: Irish McCalla, the star of the TV series *Sheena, Queen of the Jungle*, appeared with Elvis in a spoof sketch during his second appearance on *The Milton Berle Show*, which was broadcast a few months after his first appearance.

Opposite: After *The Milton Berle Show* Elvis chats to Judy Powell Spreckels, former wife of sugar heir Adolph Spreckels. They exchanged rings, leading to speculation in the Press that they were involved in a romance.

Right: After Elvis signed with RCA in 1956 he began to move away from rockabilly into true rock 'n' roll. It was the start of a gradual progression in his personal style and in his music. However, how much of this was due to a natural move onward to reach a wider audience and how much to manipulation by Colonel Parker is open to speculation.

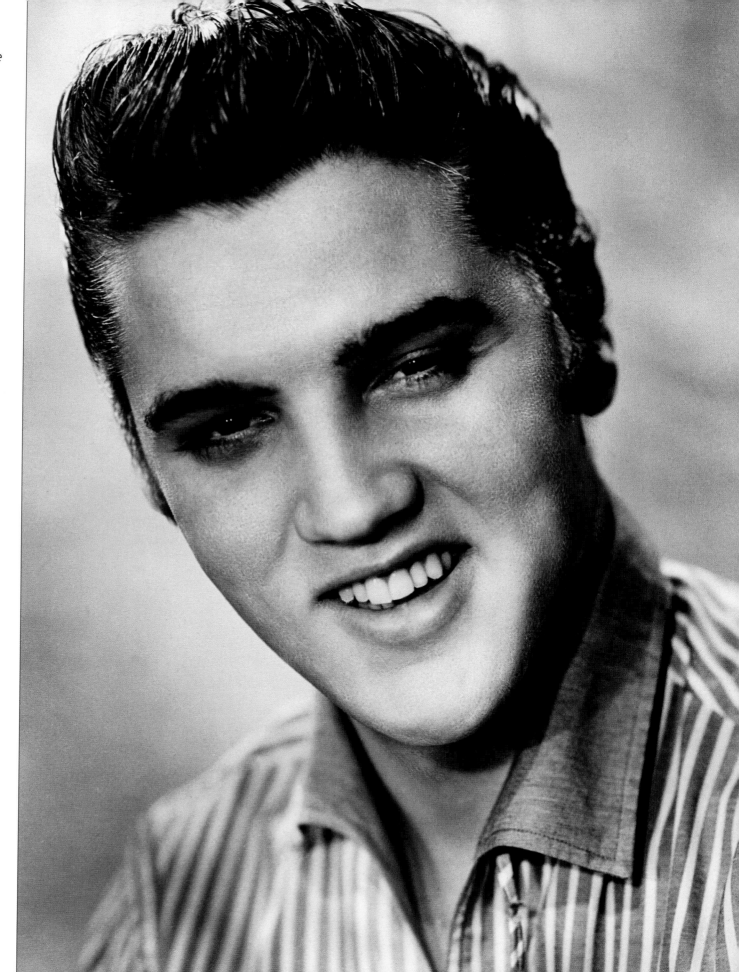

Outrageous performance

Left and opposite: It was Elvis's second appearance on *The Milton Berle Show* that caused all the controversy. During the show he sang "Hound Dog" for the first time on television. Although "Hound Dog" was a brand-new song the audience loved it and their enthusiastic reception spurred Elvis to take his hip-swiveling performance to even greater heights. As he reached the final part of the song he slowed the tempo down and began to thrust his hips in time to the music in a decidedly suggestive way.

You ain't nothing but a Hound Dog...

Left: As Elvis moved into the closing sequence of "Hound Dog" the studio audience were driven to a frenzy of excitement, screaming and laughing at the same time. That evening, for the first time in the season, *The Milton Berle Show* topped *Sergeant Bilko* in the ratings. "Hound Dog" was released in July and had sold over five million copies by the end of the year.

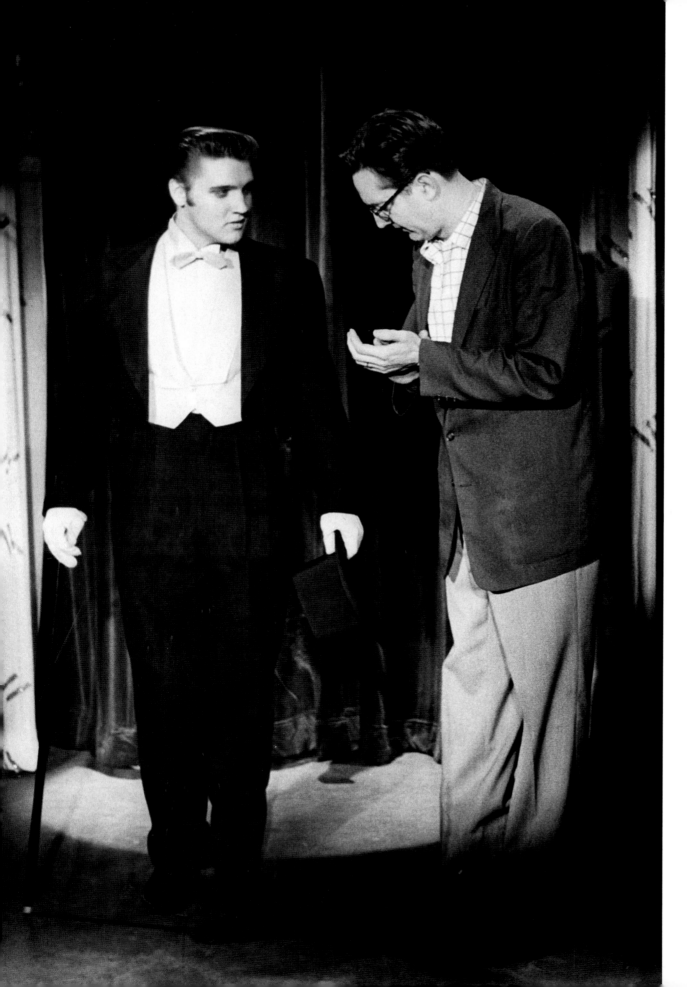

The fans protest

Left: The day after *The Milton Berle Show* was broadcast, many critics condemned Elvis's performance. Jack O'Brian of the *New York Journal-American* spoke of "… a display of primitive physical movement difficult to describe in terms suitable to a family newspaper…" and Ben Gross said in the *Daily News* that "… he gave an exhibition that was suggestive and vulgar, tinged with the kind of animalism that should be confined to dives and bordellos." Soon afterward Elvis appeared on the *Steve Allen Show (left)*, but to appease the network censors, Steve Allen insisted his performance was toned down and Elvis appeared in a tuxedo serenading a basset hound. The fans were outraged and even went so far as to picket NBC the following day.

Opposite: Elvis with girlfriend June Juanico. She was invited to stay with his family for two weeks in Memphis in 1956, but by March 1957 their relationship was over.

Playing the crowd

Left: Elvis on stage during a concert at Russwood Park in Memphis on July 4, 1956. Fourteen thousand people – mostly teenagers – packed the stands to hear him sing. By this time he had developed a new confidence and was easily able to tease the crowd without letting anything get out of hand. After the concert, Elvis was told about a little girl, Cherokee Rose, who had been in a car crash with her family on the way to the concert and he made the time to visit with her in hospital to speed her recovery.

Opposite: Elvis passionately kisses Cathy Reno (Debra Paget) in a still from his first movie, *Love Me Tender,* which began filming in August 1956. The picture was set just after the American Civil War and Elvis played Clint Reno, the youngest brother in a farming family, who marries his elder brother's girlfriend after everyone assumes the brother has been killed in the war. When he returns the family is torn apart and Clint is killed defending his brother in a fight – although to satisfy the fans, Elvis appears again under the final credits singing the title song.

Love Me Tender

Opposite: Love Me Tender was originally called *The Reno Brothers*, but a recording of Elvis singing the theme song, "Love Me Tender" – based on a Civil War ballad, "Aura Lee" – was a massive hit. It reached No.1 in the *Billboard* Top 100 even before the movie was released, so the picture was quickly retitled to tie in with the record's success. The role of Clint was the only one in Elvis's movie career that was not specifically written for him – in fact Robert Wagner was originally considered for the part.

Above: Elvis had first met Debra Paget earlier in 1956 when they had both appeared in a sketch for *The Milton Berle Show*. He had a crush on her, but she only found him "very sweet." She was already an established Hollywood star, and both she and Richard Egan – who played Clint's brother, Vance Reno – were billed above Elvis in the picture.

Ed Sullivan relents

Left: Elvis on set during filming of *The Ed Sullivan Show*. After the furore surrounding *The Milton Berle Show*, Sullivan had declared that he would never have the singer on his program, but later that year he backed down and signed up Elvis for three performances. By this time it was clear that the ratings for every show that Elvis appeared on invariably went up, so he was paid $50,000 – considerably more than the Colonel had asked for when he had first approached Sullivan and been turned down. The section of the first show featuring Elvis was recorded in Hollywood, where he was filming *Love Me Tender*. Ironically this particular show was hosted by actor Charles Laughton, since Sullivan himself was recovering from head injuries sustained in a car accident.

Above: With his guitar slung casually over his shoulder, Elvis studies cue cards prepared for his first appearance on *The Ed Sullivan Show*. The audience for the program was predominantly middle-aged and staid but Sullivan was out to pull in a younger generation as well. For the first two shows, broadcast in September and October 1956, Elvis was shown in his full glory. However, for his third performance, broadcast in January 1957, Sullivan decided to handle the growing controversy about Elvis's hip movements by showing him playing from the waist up only.

Opposite: Elvis at the piano with the sheet music for "Love Me Tender" during the filming of the first Sullivan show in September 1956. Although he rarely played in public, he was an accomplished pianist. He usually played just for himself or for close friends, and only when he felt happy and at ease. He often chose gospel music for pleasure, but rockabilly, and later rock 'n' roll, was what the audience wanted.

A record audience

Left: Backed by the Jordanaires, with Scotty Moore, D.J. Fontana on drums and Bill Black on bass, Elvis was relaxed and happy since he enjoyed appearing before an audience. On the first show he sang "Don't Be Cruel," "Hound Dog," "Reddy Teddy," and "Love Me Tender." The show was viewed by a record sixty million people, which at the time was 82.6 percent of the television audience in the United States, and was the largest single audience in television history.

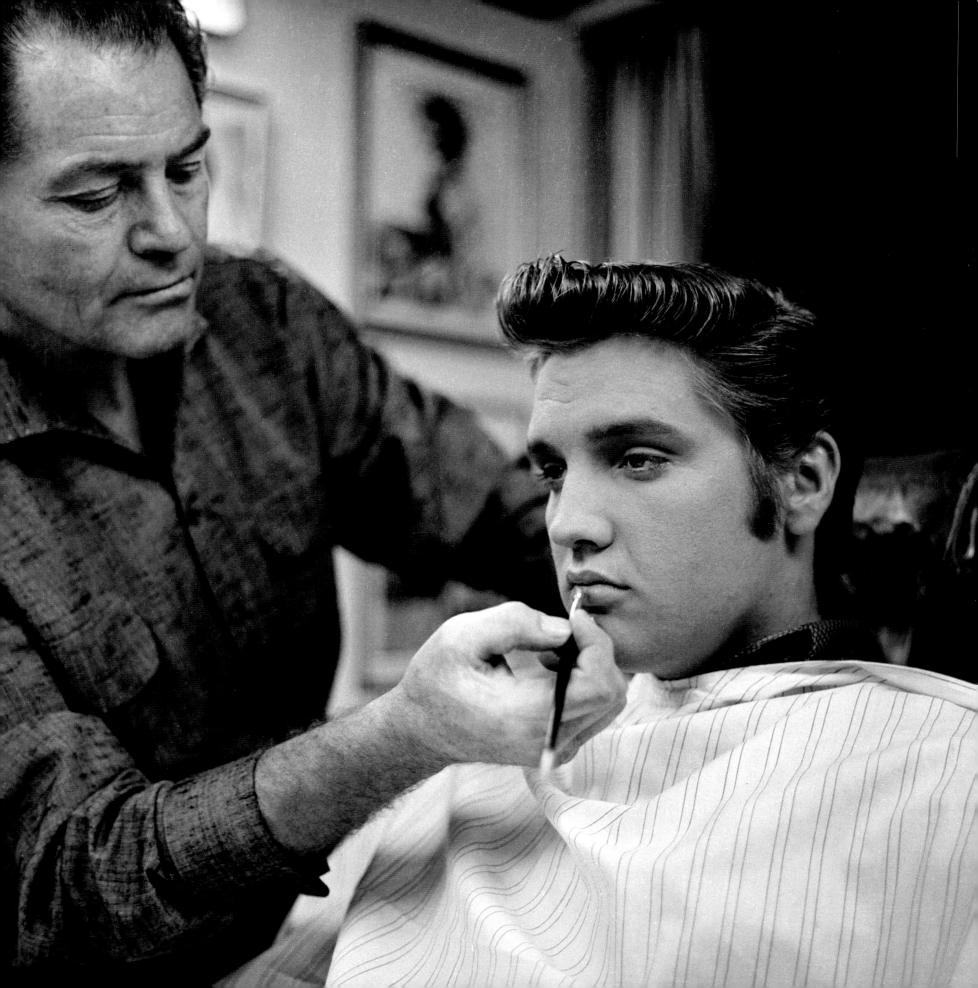

Opposite: Elvis being made up for his first appearance on *The Ed Sullivan Show.* At this stage his hair was still its natural light brown, but soon afterward it was dyed jet black, because it was thought that this would look much better on film for his movie roles. It remained the darker color for the rest of his life.

Above: Ed Sullivan discusses a few points with Elvis before his appearance on the second show, broadcast in October 1956.

A real decent, fine boy...

Above: On the second show Elvis sang the same songs as on the previous program, with the exception of "Reddy Teddy." For the last show he sang a total of seven songs, including "Heartbreak Hotel" and "Peace in the Valley." After his last number, Sullivan thanked him, saying, "This is a real decent, fine boy. We've never had a pleasanter experience on our show with a big name than we've had with you... You're thoroughly all right."

Opposite: Ed Sullivan converses with the Colonel before the filming of the second show, while Elvis adjusts his trademark hairstyle.

Keeping the fans happy

Opposite: Elvis signs autographs for his fans backstage at the second Sullivan show, which was recorded in New York. The Colonel always had a supply of photographs for them to buy and Elvis was always happy to sign. In later years he rarely went out in public as he was constantly mobbed.

Above: Backed by the Jordanaires and with Bill Black on bass in the background, Elvis shakes a leg for the girls in the audience. Black often played the fool with his bass, pretending to dance with it or to ride it like a horse – which frequently raised a laugh. Elvis had recently received a Gold disk for "Love Me Tender," his fifth for that year. Even before the record was released in early October 1956, RCA had advance orders for one million copies.

Above: The day before the second Sullivan show was broadcast, *Billboard* had caused Elvis fans to panic by announcing that the Army planned to give him a GI haircut. Elvis had received his draft questionnaire at the beginning of October, but he seemed unconcerned about the impending loss of his bouffant locks.

Opposite: Elvis with his Martin D-28 guitar, which had a custom-made tooled leather cover. Although he had others, he used this guitar most for performing and recording until he got a Gibson J200 in October 1956.

Committed to their careers

Opposite: Elvis met Natalie Wood when they were introduced by Nick Adams, an actor who became his friend when he was in Hollywood working on *Love Me Tender*. He and Natalie got on well and dated for a while, but despite Press rumors of wedding bells the relationship came to nothing. Natalie told journalists that they were both too committed to their careers to think about marriage.

Right: Always generous with his time, Elvis is pictured chatting to two convalescent teenagers during a visit to a hospital in the late 1950s.

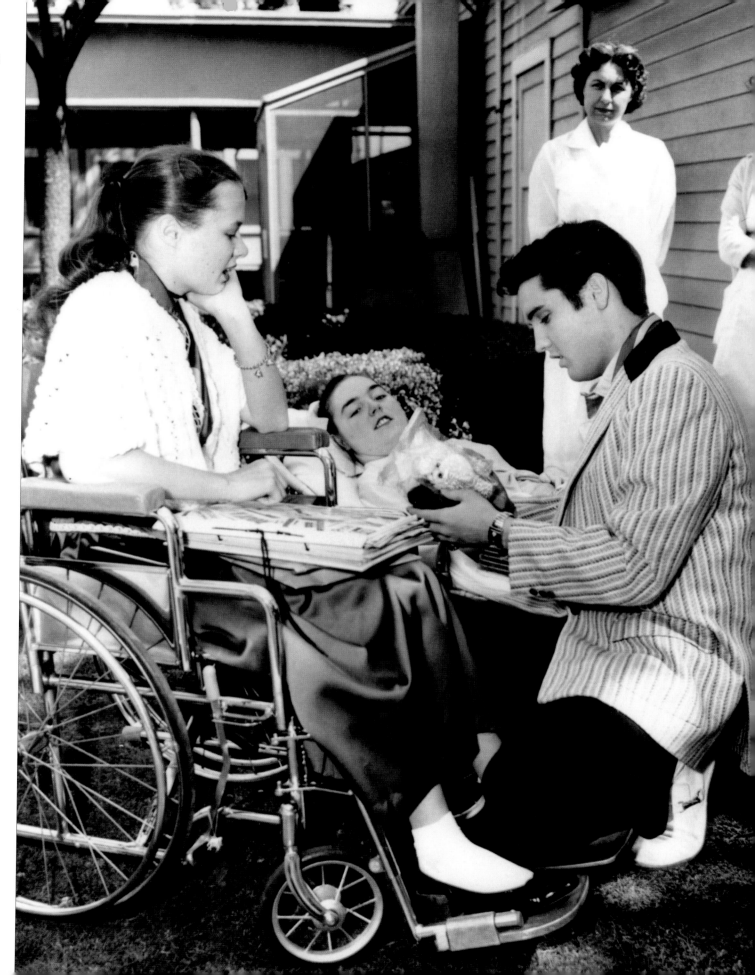

New York, 1956

Opposite: When *Love Me Tender* was released in November 1956 it was panned by the critics – unsurprisingly given the bad press Elvis had received that year. They were particularly scathing of his performance, but in fact for an inexperienced actor he had done very well. He had memorized all his lines and was willing to learn and take direction, but Producer David Weisbart felt that his greatest asset was his natural ability, even going as far as to compare him with James Dean.

Right: A studio portrait of Elvis, taken toward the end of 1956.

Liberace and Elvis

Left and Opposite: On the opening night of Liberace's concert at the Riviera in Las Vegas in November 1956, Elvis had a front-row seat. He was taking a few days off and staying at the New Frontier Hotel. After the concert Liberace and Elvis swopped jackets and instruments and fooled around for the cameras. Liberace's jacket was a gold cutaway, and was the inspiration for the famous $2,500 gold-lamé suit that RCA gave Elvis the following April. The Colonel had it made up by Nudie Cohen's Rodeo Tailors in Hollywood, and Elvis wore it for the first time in March 1957 for a concert in Kiel Auditorium, St. Louis.

Memphis Mafia

Left: By the beginning of 1957, Elvis was accompanied by armed security guards wherever he went, since he could no longer so much as step into the street without causing a riot. He was constantly surrounded by members of his entourage, a close-knit circle of men who were both companions and support group. They rushed to fulfill every whim and sometimes fueled his ego. Often appearing badly-behaved and arrogant to outsiders, they became known as the "Memphis Mafia."

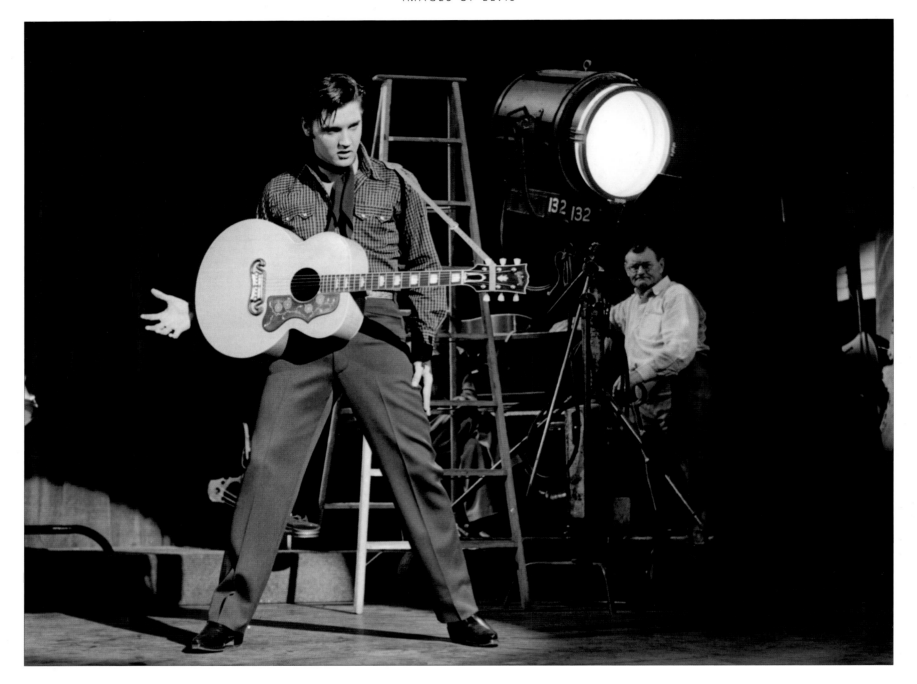

Loving You

Above: Elvis on the set of *Loving You* in 1957. His parents had come out to Hollywood to see him at work and were persuaded to appear in one scene, watching the concert at the climax of the story. After his mother died, Elvis was never able to bring himself to watch the movie again.

Opposite: The storyline of *Loving You* was loosely based on Elvis's own life. An unknown, but talented, singer with a new sound is discovered by a hard-headed promoter – although in the picture the promoter is female and played by Lizabeth Scott. At first Deke Rivers – Elvis's character – appeals to teenage audiences, but the Press label him as a bad influence. After Deke proves that he is really a fine, upstanding young man, the movie ends happily.

Love interest

Opposite: Elvis with Dolores Hart, who played Susan Jessup, the young girl his character falls in love with in *Loving You*. Dolores also appeared in *King Creole* in a similar role. She made only a few more movies before entering a convent and taking her vows to become a nun.

Left: Elvis on set. Just before filming started on *Loving You* on January 21, he had reported to the Kennedy Veterans Hospital in Memphis for his pre-induction US Army physical. He was classed 1-A, which meant he was eligible for military service – although the Army confirmed that he was unlikely to be called up for at least six months.

Above: Elvis in New York in 1957. One of the first purchases he had made with his new-found wealth was a home for his parents in Audubon Drive, Memphis. Unfortunately fans often arrived in their hundreds to hang around outside, and the neighbors soon tired of this constant intrusion. Elvis decided he needed a property with some seclusion, so Vernon and Gladys set out to find one. As soon as they saw Graceland in March 1957 they fell in love with it, and quickly called Elvis to come and see it for himself.

Opposite: Despite working on publicizing his new movie career, Elvis was still performing regularly, but it was becoming somewhat hazardous to attend his concerts because of the wild behavior of some of the fans.

Pistols at dawn...

Right: Elvis got himself into trouble when he was accused of pulling a gun on Private First Class Hershel, after the young marine claimed Elvis had insulted his wife. Since Elvis had never met Mrs Hershel – and the gun was a prop, which he had brought back from Hollywood – the whole affair was settled out of court. The attentions of unknown females were an occupational hazard – in November 1956 an unemployed steelworker, Louis Balint, was fined for attacking Elvis because his wife's passion for the singer had broken up their marriage.

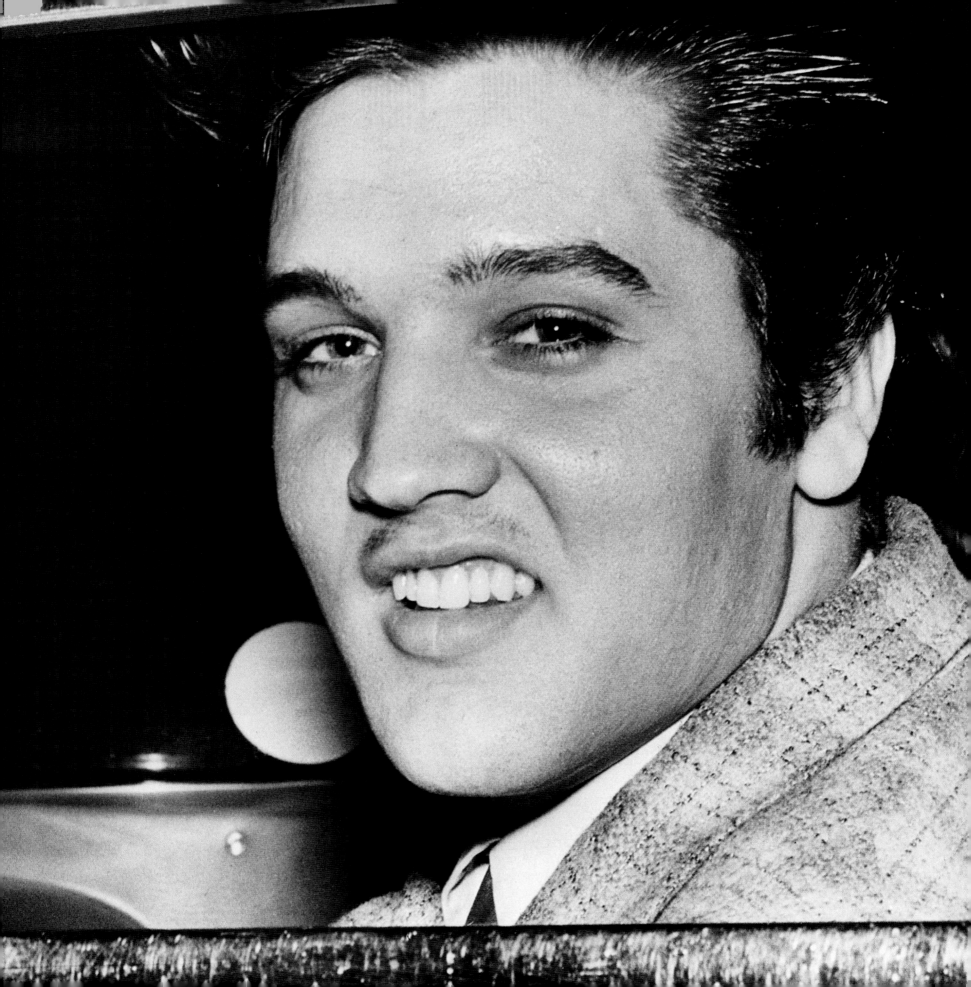

Jailhouse Rock

Right: Elvis's third movie, *Jailhouse Rock*, began filming in May 1957. In it he played Vince Edwards, a backwoods boy with a hot temper, who kills a man in self-defense in a fight and is sent to prison. The picture featured songs specially commissioned from Leiber and Stoller, who came out to Hollywood to oversee the recording. Unfortunately, the Colonel insisted that the writers of all Elvis's songs had to hand over a percentage of their royalties. Word soon got around, seriously limiting the selection of songs that Elvis was offered in later years – to the point that it began to damage his career.

Opposite: During a particularly energetic dance routine for *Jailhouse Rock*, Elvis swallowed one of the temporary crowns from his teeth. It lodged in his lung and had to be recovered by inserting an instrument through his vocal cords. He was hoarse for a few days afterward and there was some concern that his voice would be permanently affected, but the fears proved to be groundless.

Left: During the shooting of the movie Elvis dated one of his co-stars – Anne Neyland, a former Miss Texas.

Tragic co-star

Right: Judy Tyler and Elvis in *Jailhouse Rock*.
Judy played Peggy van Alden, a record
promoter who helps Vince to stardom after he
is released from prison. They got on very well
during filming, but Judy was newly married
and not interested in romance. Tragically, she
and her husband were killed in an accident
shortly after filming was completed. Elvis was
distraught and did not go to the premiere or
watch the movie in later years.

Professional style

Left: For the big dance sequence performed to the title song, Elvis was backed by a team of professional dancers. Choreographer Alex Romero watched Elvis move around naturally when he was singing, then worked up the steps into a routine. During filming Elvis became friendly with professional dancer Russ Tamblyn, who gave him a few tips to sharpen up his dancing style.

Opposite: The plot of the movie had Elvis being taught to sing and play by a cellmate while he is in jail. He soon becomes a star after his release, but treats both his former cellmate and Peggy, his record promoter, with disdain, until an accident stops him in his tracks. After he becomes a reformed character, he and Peggy fall in love.

Black and white

Opposite: Jailhouse Rock was a low-budget movie shot in black and white, with stylized sets, but the simple settings enhanced the serious storyline. Many believe it was one of the best movies Elvis ever made – and it made a great deal of money for MGM and for Elvis himself, who received a percentage of the profits.

Right: The single "Jailhouse Rock"/"Treat Me Nice" from the soundtrack was the first Elvis record to enter the charts at No.1 in the UK, in September 1957. It went on to sell three million copies in twelve months.

Summer 1957

Left: Elvis checks his hair. After filming of *Jailhouse Rock* was completed, he embarked on a tour of the Pacific Northwest, covering five cities in four days. At a concert in the Memorial Stadium in Spokane, 12,000 fans were whipped into a frenzy and afterward some tried to steal soil from the infield because his feet had touched it.

Opposite: Anita Wood says goodbye to Elvis as he prepares to leave on his trip. She was a former beauty queen whom he first saw on *Top Ten Dance Party* on WHBQ, and dated for several years. Although he also saw other women during their relationship it was fairly serious – she was a regular visitor to Graceland and got on well with his mother. He gave her a sapphire and diamond ring, which she told reporters was merely a friendship ring – although privately both she and others thought it was much more.

Drafted!

Opposite: In December 1957 Elvis finally received his draft notification. He told reporters that he was happy to return something to the country that had given him so much.

Right: Elvis gets his pre-induction medical from Dr Fred Jeff Burford in March 1958. He had been given a sixty-day deferment to allow him to finish filming *King Creole*, as otherwise the studio would have lost the large sum of money already spent on pre-production.

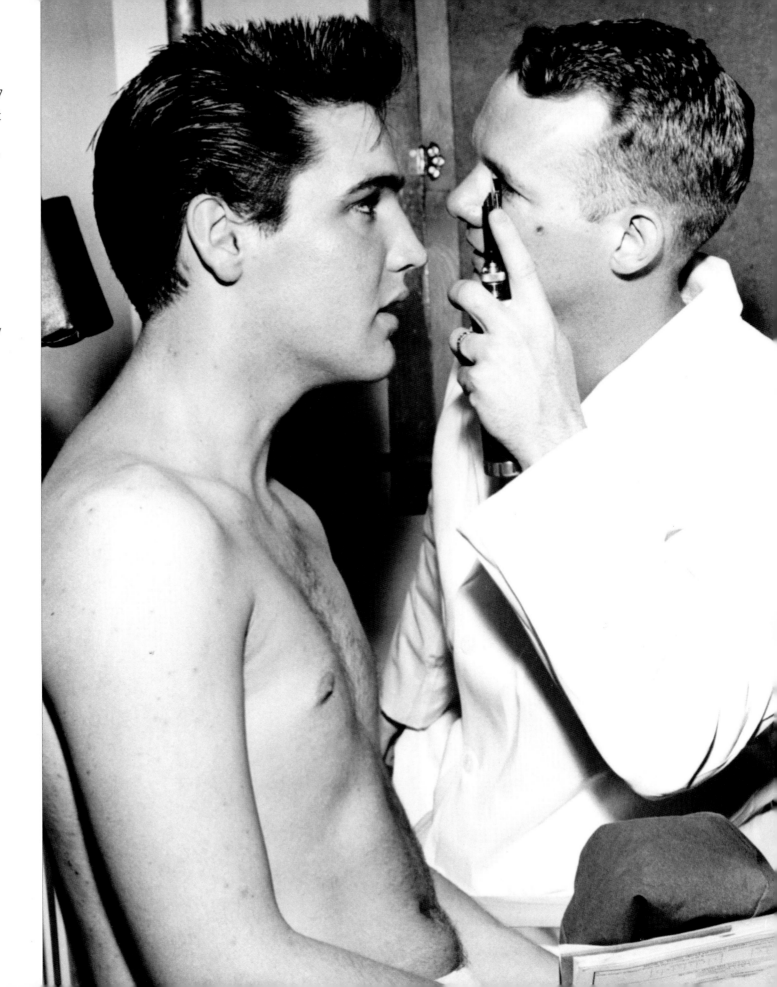

A new career

Right: Elvis bids farewell to Vernon and Gladys. Representatives from the military authorities had offered him special status: the Navy planned to form a company round him that would entertain the troops; the Air Force suggested he could spend his time touring recruiting centers. Elvis turned down their offers, saying he just wanted to be treated like everyone else. Privately he was concerned that two years away would cause the fans to forget him and end his career. However, the Colonel was nothing if not resourceful – he knew that there was a stock of unreleased material that could keep things ticking over in his boy's absence, and he intended to take full advantage of the PR opportunities offered by such a big star buckling down to serve his country.

March 1958

Opposite: There were fifty-five reporters and photographers on hand to record the famous Army haircut. Elvis held up some of the hair for the Press and joked, "Hair today, gone tomorrow!"

Left: Major Elbert P. Turner swears in Elvis and other recruits at the draft board in Memphis. Afterward they were taken by bus to Fort Chaffee in Arkansas, followed by a troupe of Press from around the world. The Press were constantly present with the Army's permission – but after one photographer hid in the barracks at Fort Chaffee to try to get a picture of Elvis sleeping in his bunk it was decided that things had gone too far and the hapless snapper was ejected.

JAMES B. PETERSON
MANAGER

A new look Elvis

Right: All the publicity surrounding the haircut so flustered Elvis that he forgot to pay the 65-cent fee to the barber and had to be called back, much to his embarrassment.

Opposite: Just before the haircut Elvis ran a comb through his locks and told the Press that he was dreading the forthcoming shearing. As well as medical tests and a haircut he also had to complete five hours of aptitude tests and sit through a two-hour lecture on a private's rights and privileges.

All-American boy...

Opposite: At Fort Chaffee Elvis was photographed making his bed, having breakfast and being issued with and wearing his uniform. He was then assigned to Fort Hood in Texas for basic training, where he was also to receive advanced tank instruction.

Right: Having seen the circus at Fort Chaffee, those in charge at Fort Hood decided on a different approach. After one day of unrestricted access, the new recruit was strictly off limits. It was the first time that Elvis had been away from his family and friends, but he buckled down to learning how to be a soldier.

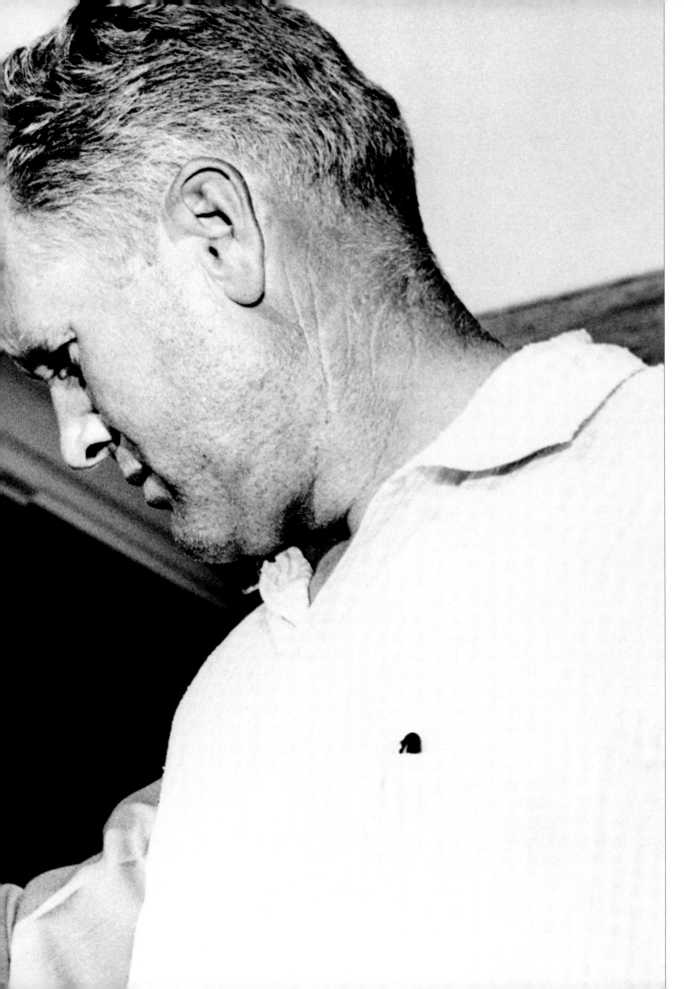

Just the same as everyone else

Left: On his first furlough in May 1958, Elvis returned to Graceland to see his family. On his arrival, Vernon admired his son's medals. Elvis had earned his marksman medal with a carbine and his sharpshooter medal with a pistol and was now acting assistant squad leader. He told reporters that he had gradually been accepted by the others – he had never asked for anything and just did the same as everyone else. He had fourteen days' leave, part of which was spent recording in Nashville so that RCA would have some new material to release while he was away.

Inconsolable

Right: After the Colonel discovered that a soldier could live off base if he had dependants in the area, Vernon and Gladys moved to Killeen, the nearest town to Fort Hood. They rented a house and Elvis drove back and forth to the base each day. However, Gladys was feeling increasingly ill and the hot Texas summer was not helping. In August she returned to Memphis to see her doctor, who rushed her to hospital. Despite many tests it was unclear what the problem was, but it was obviously serious. Elvis was given compassionate leave to return to Memphis to see his mother. Although she appeared to rally when Elvis arrived, Gladys died of a heart attack two days later. Elvis was inconsolable and told the Press that his mother's death had broken his heart.

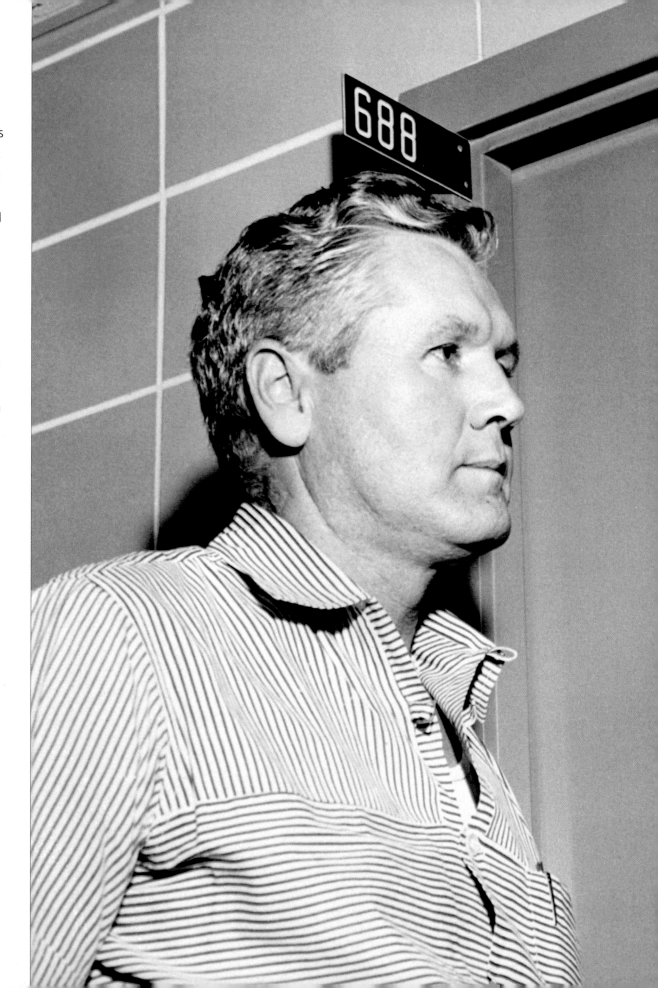

September '58: Off to Germany

Left: Little more than a month after his mother's funeral, Elvis's unit left for Germany. Although he had never been in Europe he already had fans there: at least 500 teenagers arrived to welcome him when his ship docked at Bremerhaven. From there, the soldiers caught a train to the base at Friedberg, near Frankfurt.

In October 1958 Bill Haley appeared in concert in Frankfurt and Elvis went to see him, although he had to stay backstage to avoid causing a riot. He told Haley that he was grateful for his help and encouragement in the early days, as without it he might still be driving a truck.

Rocking the night away

Opposite: Elvis shaving at base camp in Grafenwöhr while on maneuvers. In Germany he had been assigned to Company C, a scout platoon, where he drove a jeep for Reconnaissance Platoon Sergeant Ira Jones. One of the reasons that Company C was selected was because it spent much of its time on maneuvers, so Private Presley could be kept out of the public eye. He proved himself to be a resourceful and clever scout, soon earning the acceptance both of his sergeant and the other men.

Left: Elvis reads a letter from home during his stay in Germany.

Sergeant Presley

Opposite: Elvis had previously been promoted to Specialist Fourth Class, but in January 1960 he was promoted again to acting sergeant. He proudly showed off his stripes to photographers. The promotion brought no increase in pay, but since Sergeant Presley was considerably richer than most soldiers, this did not concern him!

Above: While he was in Germany, Elvis bought a second-hand white BMW 507 sports car. He did not stay on base – his father, grandmother, and a couple of the Memphis Mafia had come out too and they rented a house nearby so Elvis could live with them. However, Elvis did mix with army personnel and met the young Priscilla Beaulieu at a party in November 1959.

Public Enemy No.1

Left: Russian leaders dubbed Sergeant Presley "Public Enemy Number One," accusing the US of using him as a weapon in psychological warfare.

Opposite: During the time he was in Germany, Elvis never once appeared on stage or sang for a proper audience. He had been instructed not to do so by Colonel Tom Parker – partly so that he would not be treated differently from the other men, but also because the Colonel did not see why the Army should get for free what everyone else was prepared to pay a fortune for. Meanwhile, the Colonel was negotiating to set up new deals ready for his boy's return.

Time to go home

Above: March 1960 and Elvis faces a last Press conference in Germany before leaving for the US. He told newsmen that he had learned a lot in the Army and he made several new friends – including Charlie Hodge, who came to work for him in civilian life and stayed to the end, and, of course, Priscilla who was delighted to find that Elvis did not forget his promise to keep in touch with her.

Opposite: Back in the US Elvis boards a bus at Fort Dix to take him from the orientation lecture to the base finance building to collect his final pay packet. He looked smart and well turned out as always – he had purchased several spare sets of kit, which the Memphis Mafia looked after for him. The media interest in his return proved that the fans had not forgotten him.

Paying his dues

Above: When Elvis received a last Army pay packet the Colonel reminded him not to forget his manager's commission, so Elvis handed over the whole $109.54. The entire homecoming was carefully orchestrated to achieve the most publicity for the returning soldier.

Opposite: At a Press conference, lucky fan Barbara Ann Murray of Roselle Park, New Jersey, gets more than she bargained for when she approaches Elvis for an autograph: not only his signature, but also a kiss and to sit on his lap for the cameras. Although Elvis told newsmen he was looking forward to some time off, he actually had a busy schedule lined up.

Elvis, we still love you!

Above: Finally Elvis signed some autographs for a few Army buddies, then at last he was free to rejoin civilian life. He had told some of his friends that he was looking forward to making more movies, and hoped to get a few more serious roles. The Colonel had several contracts lined up, as well as a recording session and an appearance on *The Frank Sinatra Show* to be recorded in Miami.

Opposite: As well as appearing with Sinatra in the spring of 1960, Elvis recorded some of his classic hits – including "Are You Lonesome Tonight?" and "It's Now or Never," which went on to sell nine million copies. The LP *Elvis is Back* stayed in the *Billboard* chart for fifty-six weeks. The fans soon resumed their old habits, and Elvis was besieged wherever he went.

GI Blues

Right: In May 1960 Elvis began filming *GI Blues*, a musical comedy in which he played a singer serving in the Army. The story borrowed heavily from recent events in his own life – his character is not only stationed in Germany, but is also in a tank division. The movie was aimed at a more general market, rather than just being for teenagers, and Elvis appears more mature and responsible. The picture also starred Juliet Prowse, the current girlfriend of Frank Sinatra. All the scenes featuring Elvis were shot in Hollywood, with the location shots in Germany done at another time.

Royalty meets the King

Right: While filming of *GI Blues* was in progress, a steady stream of important visitors came to the set. Here Elvis chats to three Scandinavian princesses, but on the same day he had also welcomed the King and Queen of Thailand and the wife and daughter of the Brazilian president, as well as Pat Boone, Minnie Pearl and Ernie Ford. The Colonel was responsible for the Royals – he was tireless when it came to promoting "his boy." Despite all the interruptions the final movie was a tremendous success, both with the critics and at the box office. It seemed that everyone approved of his new image, but Elvis worried that the musical numbers did not fit into the plot very well, and that the songs were not as good as in some of his previous pictures. Despite this, the soundtrack album soon reached No.1 and stayed in the charts for longer than any of his others.

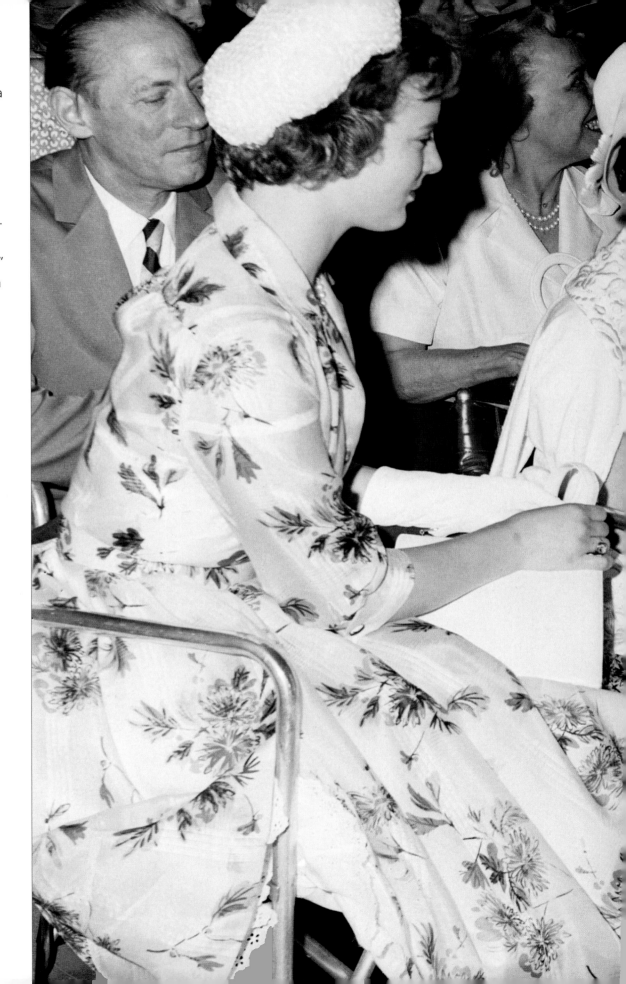

A new direction

Above: Chief Wah-Nee-Ota inducts Elvis into the Los Angeles Tribal Council in recognition of his role in *Flaming Star*. This movie marked a new direction for Elvis as it had a serious storyline, a respected director – Don Siegel – and a cast of notable actors. There were only two songs in the final released version, which disappointed the fans so although it was a critical success it did not do so well at the box office as previous movies.

Opposite: Although his hair soon grew out of the regulation Army short back and sides, Elvis never again wore it in the long duck-tail that had been his trademark in pre-Army days.

Another serious role

Opposite: Although he made it without incident through all the rough and tumble while filming *Flaming Star*, Elvis broke his finger playing touch football between takes.

Right: Only a month after filming finished in October, Elvis began work on his next movie, *Wild in the Country*. This again had fewer songs and a more serious story – Elvis played Glenn Tyler, who is released from a juvenile institution determined to sort out his life. As with *Flaming Star* it did less well at the box office, so Elvis was persuaded to go back to musical comedy.

January 1961: Blue Hawaii

Above: Elvis as Chad Gates in *Blue Hawaii*, with Roland Winters as his father, Fred Gates. Angela Lansbury was cast as his mother, Sarah Lee Gates, although she was only thirty-five at the time. *Blue Hawaii* had fourteen songs, a lightweight story and lots of shots of beautiful scenery. It was a massive success, so it set the direction for Elvis's movies in the future. A song from the soundtrack, "Can't help Falling in Love," was released as a single in October 1961 and was a big hit for Elvis.

Opposite: A cluster of fans surrounds Elvis in Los Angeles airport as he prepares to leave for filming on Hawaii. He stayed for three weeks on the island, during which time he also gave several benefit performances. In the picture his character has just returned from the Army and his parents are trying to get him to join the family fruit business. Instead he becomes a tour guide, which gives director Norman Taurog plenty of opportunity to feature beautiful girls, tourist hotspots, and the odd serenade.

On the beach...

Left: Joan Blackman played the love interest and they looked good on screen together – although there were rumors that they did not get on so well off screen. Elvis was apprehensive about working in deep water, but bravely faced his fear so most of the scenes were shot as planned. Although *Blue Hawaii* was so successful, in many ways it was bad for Elvis's future movie career. He was not required to display any technical acting skill – he had been reduced to appearing as an attractive presence on the screen. Many of the later pictures tried to reproduce the formula with varying degrees of success.

Opposite: Elvis with co-star Joanne Moore in *Follow That Dream*, which began shooting in July 1961 in Florida. The script was decent and Elvis gave a good performance as idiot-savant Toby Kwimper, displaying a flair for comedy.

Late for the wedding

Right: Elvis got lost on his way to the wedding of his secretary, Pat Boyd, to one of the Memphis Mafia, Bobby "Red" West on July 1, 1961. Elvis was to be the best man, but he missed the ceremony so someone else had to stand in. He arrived in time for the reception, after which he had rented the Memphis Fairground Amusement Park from midnight to 6.30 a.m. the following morning for all the wedding guests to enjoy. Red West had been the driver when Elvis and the Blue Moon Boys had toured back in 1955, and after the Army he had come back as one of Elvis's bodyguards. After several incidents in which he was heavy-handed with aggressive fans in 1976, he was fired by Vernon Presley and became an actor and stuntman.

It Happened at the World's Fair

Right: Elvis and Joan O'Brien play patient and nurse in Norman Taurog's *It Happened at the World's Fair*. This was Elvis's twelfth movie and in it he played Mike Edwards, a young pilot who flies a cropduster in partnership with his friend Danny, played by Gary Lockwood. Because of Danny's gambling debts their plane is impounded by the local sheriff, and the two young men set off to Seattle to earn some money at the fair. Elvis meets a young nurse, Diane, played by Joan O'Brien and, of course, Mike and Diane fall in love, and after a series of adventures and misunderstandings, all ends happily.

More films in 1962

Above: In a fit of anger, Elvis slugs Jeremy Slater in *Girls! Girls! Girls!* The second of Elvis's pictures to be made in Hawaii, the movie began shooting in April 1962. It featured Otis Blackwell's "Return to Sender," which was released as a single in the following October. Although he had not seen her since he left Germany in 1960, Elvis was still in regular contact with Priscilla Beaulieu.

Opposite: Elvis gets a manicure on Seattle's monorail in September 1962. He was in the city for location filming for *It Happened at the World's Fair*, since the 1962 World's Fair was being held there at the time. That June, Priscilla had finally arrived from Germany to visit Elvis, after long negotiation with her parents since she was still only sixteen. All too soon she had to return home, but Elvis began to plan to bring her to America permanently.

Fun in Acapulco

Above: Elvis holds the hand of Swiss-born actress Ursula Andress in a still from *Fun in Acapulco*. Although some of the scenes were filmed on location in Mexico, the Colonel was opposed to Elvis working there, citing concerns for his security as the reason.

Right: Elvis looks through the camera on the set of *Fun in Acapulco*.

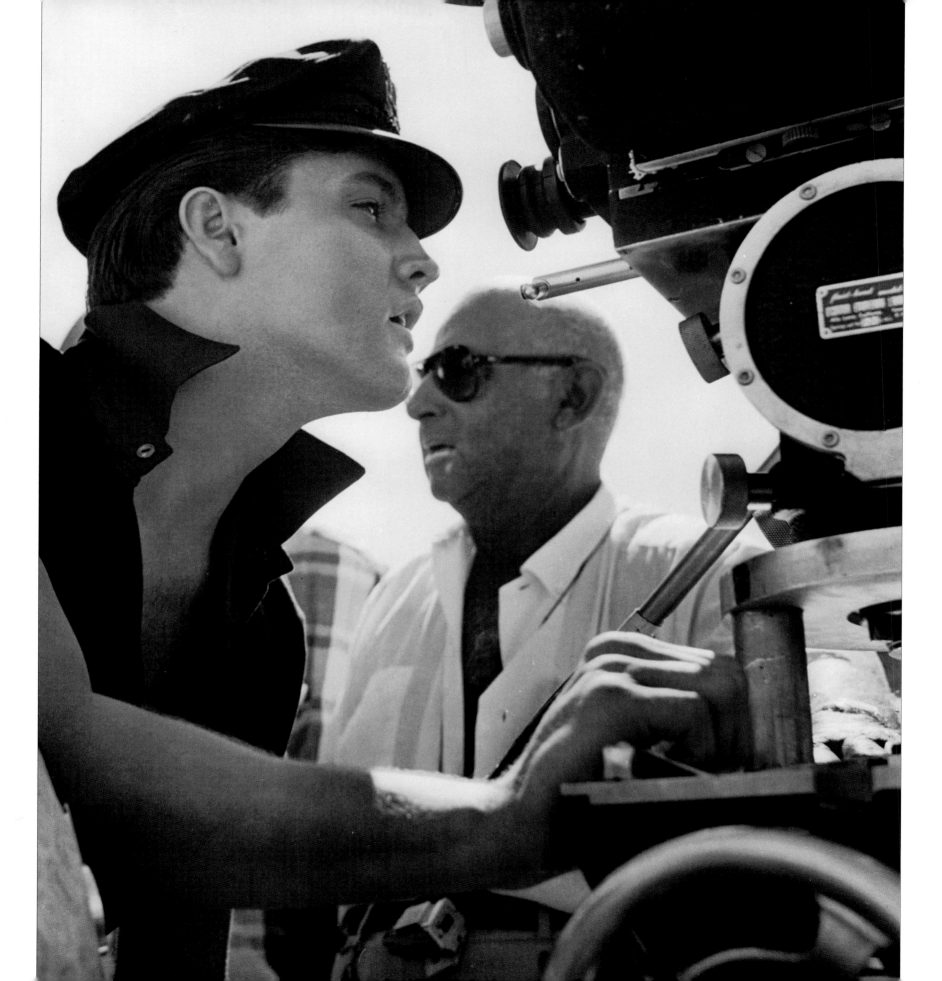

1963: Viva Las Vegas

Right: Ann-Margret and Elvis during filming of *Viva Las Vegas* for MGM in 1963. Ann-Margret was known as the "female Elvis Presley" because of her sensual performing style, and rumors swiftly began circulating that the two stars were having an affair. This time the rumors were true – although by now Priscilla was quietly living at Graceland.

A serious affair...

Left: The affair with Ann-Margret was the most serious that Elvis had with any of his co-stars. They even went on dates together without assorted members of the Memphis Mafia in tow, and many people thought they were an ideal match. However, Ann-Margret was serious about her career and certainly did not want to give it up for marriage at this stage. Elvis also had Priscilla to consider – to obtain her father's permission to bring her over to the US from Germany, he had apparently promised that they would marry one day. Of course Priscilla saw all the stories in the Press, and she was worried and confused about where her relationship with Elvis was going.

However, because of the sexual chemistry between the two stars, the musical numbers in the movie vibrate with a sensual passion. Although Elvis went straight back home after filming finished, he stayed in touch with Ann-Margret and they were close friends until he died. He always sent flowers on her opening nights.

Love duet...

Left: Elvis and Ann-Margret study the score of a song they are to sing together. The Colonel ensured that one of three planned duets was cut from the finished movie and another remade as a solo for Elvis, since he felt that too much prominence was being given to the girl in an Elvis Presley picture.

Opposite: In 1964 the Colonel decided Elvis should buy the USS *Potomac* for $55,000 and present it to the March of Dimes. Unfortunately, it was too expensive to maintain so the gift was turned down. Finally comedian Danny Thomas accepted the *Potomac* from Elvis on behalf of his charity, the St. Jude Hospital in Memphis, a research center that investigated serious childhood diseases. Elvis personally supported several local charities in Memphis and also sometimes performed benefit concerts.

Meeting James Brown

Right: While Elvis was filming *Roustabout* in March 1964, the actor James Brown popped by to say hello. By now, Elvis movies were on extremely short schedules – his previous picture, *Kissin' Cousins*, was filmed in only seventeen days. Up until then a certain standard had been maintained, but from then on it was all downhill.

Roustabout

Above: Elvis with Barbara Stanwyck in *Roustabout*. He played a carnival hand with a knack for getting into trouble, while she played the boss. Initially the two stars did not get on, but later they became friends.

Opposite: With his carnival background, it was no surprise that the Colonel had suggested the original idea and he came up with many bits of original "business," which were incorporated in the movie.

Another day, another movie

Right: Since 1960, Elvis had been making at least three movies a year with increasingly short schedules and lower production values. *Harum Scarum*, filmed in early 1965, was so poorly received that even the Colonel decided more time should be spent on the next movie. *Frankie and Johnnie (right)* was made for United Artists and was competent, but still undemanding of its star – who was visibly overweight. By this time Elvis was interested in religion, philosophy, and the occult, and he spent hours discussing books with his co-star, Donna Douglas, who was a member of the Self-Realization Fellowship. Elvis had not had a hit single for two years, but "Crying in the Chapel," released in April 1965, went into the top ten and became his first million-seller since "Return to Sender" in 1962.

Action hero

Opposite and previous pages: The typical Presley hero was a man of action, often with an interesting or unusual job, who could sing. In *Spinout*, a picture for MGM directed by Norman Taurog and filmed in early 1966, he was a racing driver. The 1929 Duesenberg in which he is supposed to enter the Santa Fe Road Race was a priceless classic car. Despite its glamorous settings and glimpses of a wealthy lifestyle, the movie did not do well at the box office. However, his new single, "Love Letters," released in June 1966 soon went straight into the top ten.

Meanwhile, although she had been kept out of the public eye, the Press were now aware that Priscilla was living at Graceland and began to speculate that she and Elvis were secretly married. Both her parents and the Colonel insisted that it was time for a decision – either they did marry, or Priscilla should move out. Elvis finally proposed just before Christmas 1966.

Left: Elvis in a musical number from the movie *Clambake* which was filmed in the spring of 1967.

May 1967

Right: On May 1,1967, Elvis and Priscilla were finally married by Nevada Supreme Court Justice David Zenoff, in a private ceremony held in a suite in the Tudor-style Aladdin Hotel in Las Vegas. Since the suite was relatively small, none of the Memphis Mafia nor their wives were invited to the actual ceremony.

A kiss for the bride

Above: After the ceremony Elvis and his new wife held a Press conference in the Aladdin Room. They kissed for the benefit of photographers. When asked why he had finally decided to marry, Elvis replied, "Well, I guess it was about time." Priscilla's stepfather, Colonel Beaulieu, told reporters that he had known from the beginning that they would marry one day.

Opposite: Priscilla shows off her three-carat diamond ring. Later she was to say that both she and Elvis were so nervous the previous night that neither had slept. They had known each other for more than seven years, and she had waited patiently at Graceland while he was away filming or recording, but now she hoped everything would change and they would be together properly as man and wife.

Happy couple...

Opposite and previous pages: More than one hundred people attended the reception, eating a buffet banquet while a string trio played romantic ballads – including some of the groom's hits. The exclusion of the Memphis Mafia from the actual ceremony had caused some resentment, and marked the beginning of disaffection in their ranks.

Right: After the reception the happy couple went to Palm Springs, but three days later left for Memphis. They spent three weeks at the Circle G Ranch, which Elvis had bought at the beginning of that year. Although most of the Memphis Mafia came too, for the most part they respected the newlyweds' privacy. Priscilla said later it was an opportunity for her to play house, and really look after her new husband.

Another reception

Right: At the end of May, Elvis and Priscilla held another reception for everyone who had not been at the first. They wore their formal clothes again, but it was a much more informal affair, which included the entire Graceland staff, all Elvis's uncles, aunts and cousins, and a whole collection of people who had worked for him, including his doctor, dentist, painter, horse trainer, and electrician.

Lisa Marie puts in an appearance

Above: Priscilla soon found she was pregnant and their daughter was born on February 1, 1968 at the Baptist Memorial Hospital in Memphis. Elvis had told people that if he had a daughter he wanted to call her Gladys, after his mother, but the new baby was named Lisa Marie.

Opposite: Elvis admires his new daughter, telling waiting newsmen that he was the happiest man in the world. After they arrived home he picked her up so much that Priscilla had to remind him to let the baby get some rest.

Returning home

Above: Four days after the birth of Lisa Marie, hundreds of fans, nurses, patients, and members of the Press were waiting to see the new family leave the hospital and drive off in a fleet of Cadillacs and Lincolns. Aware that photographers would also be waiting, Priscilla had carefully applied her make-up and a hairdresser had attended the hospital earlier that day to dress her hair into a big bouffant. She wore a bright pink mini-dress, while Elvis was dressed in blue.

Opposite: Elvis and Priscilla both look delighted to show off the new arrival to the waiting world. However, Elvis's schedule dictated that he could only stay at home for a month before he had to leave to begin filming his next movie, *Live a Little, Love a Little*, in California.

The Welsh Elvis

Right: Elvis and Priscilla visit Tom Jones backstage at his show in the Flamingo Hotel in Las Vegas. Tom Jones was often compared to an early Elvis in style – and in his appeal to the female fans. It seemed that Elvis's own career had stalled, however, as his latest movie, *Live a Little, Love a Little*, which was released in October 1968, had not done well at the box office.

Mutual respect

Right: Elvis had first met Tom Jones in Los Angeles in 1965 and they had become friends as they regarded each other with mutual respect. Elvis sometimes sang "Delilah" backstage before performances to warm up his voice. He had come to the show in Vegas because he was planning to sing live again, for the first time for many years. He told Tom that he thought their stage presence was similar, so seeing the Welsh singer perform would give him an idea of how an audience might react.

Comeback: December 1968

Left and opposite: The Colonel had arranged for a TV special to be taped before a live audience, to be broadcast before Christmas. Originally Elvis was to sing a straightforward collection of Christmas songs, but NBC producer Bob Finkel persuaded him to go for a radical change of image. Director Steve Binder put together a show that featured Elvis in black leather, belting out his rock 'n' roll hits.

A new direction

Opposite and left: Elvis looked slimmer and fitter than he had for some time, and seeing him perform the old songs with an exciting new freshness was a revelation to many, who had forgotten what he was capable of. The show was structured with different segments: a concert before a live audience, an informal "jamming" session with the Blue Moon Boys and assorted members of the Memphis Mafia, and a grand finale. The whole thing was recorded over several days in June.

Guitar Man

Above: "*The Comeback Special*" was not just a collection of songs – it told the story of a young man leaving home, searching for happiness and a career, the obstacles he faces and then the eventual journey back home. The song "Guitar Man" was the link between the different scenes. Elvis was concerned about the informal session because he feared that he would not be able to think of anything to say or do without a script to follow, but in the event it all fell into place once they began recording.

Opposite: Designer Bill Belew came up with a series of costumes, including a soft silk shirt with a scarf at the neck instead of a necktie – and the famous black leather suit. He went on to design for Elvis for the remainder of his life, and was responsible for the iconic jumpsuits of the 1970s.

If I Can Dream

The Colonel had insisted that the finale should be a Christmas song, but everyone felt that it would be an anticlimax after the excitement of the rest of the show. At the last minute director Steve Binder asked the vocal arranger, Earl Brown, to write a new song that would express everything that Elvis believed in. The result was "If I Can Dream," which Elvis sang with a full orchestral backing. By January 1969 the new song was No. 12 in the charts, and it went on to become yet another million-seller.

A triumph

Opposite: Elvis wore a white suit for the finale, belting out the song with such feeling that his voice almost broke on the last note. However, the Colonel was irate when he saw the first rough cut of the show, demanding to know where the Christmas song was. "Blue Christmas" was quickly added, replacing the much more dynamic "Tiger Man," but "If I Can Dream" remained the closing number.

Right: Elvis was nervous before the recording sessions in front of a real audience, since it was seven years since he had played live. He also cared deeply that the show should work, as he wanted to escape the relentless schedule of making movies and return to touring again. When *"The Comeback Special"* was broadcast, it was seen by 42 percent of the viewing audience, making it the No. 1 show of the season.

Back to Vegas

Left and opposite: In the summer of 1969, after the success of his comeback show, Elvis performed a series of dates at the newly-opened International Hotel in Las Vegas. At a Press conference after the first show, Elvis told reporters that he was really glad to be back in front of a live audience. There was no doubt that he was back on top – the previous night he had received four standing ovations.

That's how it was in 1970 ...

Right: Bob Abel and Pierre Adidge, the filmmakers who made *Elvis: That's The Way It Is*, approached Elvis as if he were a folk hero on a mythical journey. They were deeply involved in their subject and had the latest mobile cameras and equipment, which brought movement and spontaneity to the filming. At the outset they told Elvis that they wanted to shoot the real him and that if they felt he was posing or playing up they would simply turn off the cameras. Elvis appreciated their honesty and was committed to the project. The film included fascinating backstage material and candid shots, but Elvis is obviously not as fit, healthy, and vibrantly alive as he had appeared in *"The Comeback Special"* just two years earlier.

Putting on a good show

Above: Elvis was not only best man at the wedding of his old friend George Klein in Las Vegas in December 1970, he also paid for the whole affair. In addition, he flew half a dozen of his entourage to Las Vegas and paid for them to stay with him at the International. Here he poses for cameras with the blushing bride. Klein was a former DJ and member of the Memphis Mafia and had appeared in small parts in many of Elvis's movies.

Opposite: Elvis, Priscilla, and singer Glen Campbell at the Klein wedding. Glen Campbell had once worked as a session singer for Elvis, and they had gone on to become good friends.

No smoke ...

Opposite: Elvis indulges in a cigarillo. Although he never smoked cigarettes, Elvis was very fond of the occasional miniature cigar.

Right: A passionate kiss for the cameras. Although their marriage was already in trouble, both Elvis and Priscilla were adept at putting on a good show in public. Although many of the Memphis Mafia were now married, the women very rarely got into the picture. Elvis had banned them from coming on tour, which also meant that Priscilla could not accompany him. Her continued absence from his side was explained publicly as being due to the work she was involved in overseeing the new house being built in Monovale Drive in Beverly Hills, California.

Lawman ...

Opposite: Elvis proudly displays one of his guns. He had built up quite a collection and even walked down the aisle as best man at Sonny West's wedding in Memphis wearing two guns in a shoulder holster, two pearl-handled pistols in the waistband of his pants and a derringer in his boot.

Above: Elvis not only collected guns but also badges, and in October 1970 he had been sworn in as a special deputy – along with many members of the Memphis Mafia – so he could carry a handgun.

At the White House

Above and opposite: After meeting voice-over artist Paul Frees and learning that he worked as an undercover narcotics agent – complete with an official Bureau of Narcotics and Dangerous Drugs badge – Elvis was determined to get a BNDD badge himself. He failed to obtain one from the Bureau, but undeterred he simply offered his services in the fight against drugs to President Nixon. An invitation to the White House swiftly followed – along with the coveted badge. Elvis was so overjoyed he stepped forward and hugged Nixon – catching both the President and his aide off guard.

On Tour

Opposite: Throughout 1969 to 1977 Elvis was almost constantly giving concerts or touring. Although he told people he would like to do relaxed and laid-back shows, he knew the audience expected him to throw all his energy into a performance. At first this was easy and enjoyable, but after a while the constant traveling, coupled with his growing dependence on prescription drugs, began to take its toll on his health.

Above: A relaxed and smiling Elvis.

188

Opposite: The jumpsuits Elvis wore while performing were mainly designed by Bill Belew and they became increasingly elaborate; sometimes they incorporated a cape – either waist or floor length – and they were decorated with gemstones and semi-precious jewels. The symbols used on some of the later suits were significant to Elvis – eagles, karate symbols, tigers, and peacocks, and the fans gave these outfits special names.

Above: Priscilla, Lisa Marie and Elvis in an official portrait to mark Lisa Marie's third birthday. Despite the appearance of being a happy family, Priscilla was already becoming dissatisfied with their marriage.

Daddy's Girl

Opposite: Elvis adored his daughter and named one of his private aircraft the *Lisa Marie*. Despite this he was away on tour often while she was growing up.

Above: To make up for his constant absences, Elvis bought Lisa Marie expensive gifts, including a mink coat and a diamond ring, but Priscilla often deemed them inappropriate for a little girl and took them away after the doting father had left again.

Mother and daughter

Opposite: Despite the appearance of closeness, Priscilla had recently become involved with martial arts expert Mike Stone, whom she had first met in Hawaii with Elvis in 1968. Afterward she had become interested in karate, encouraged by Elvis, and had bumped into Stone at tournaments. Although at first their meetings were casual, over time the two of them had become close.

Left: Lisa Marie lived with her mother in California most of the time, but they came to Graceland when Elvis was there for Christmas and holidays.

New York June 1972

Opposite: At a press conference in New York, where he was appearing for the first time at Madison Square Garden, Elvis soon won over the jaded newsmen. When asked how he thought he had managed to outlast every other performer from his generation, he quickly quipped, "I take vitamin E."

Right: Another reporter asked Elvis if he was happy with his image, but Elvis pointed out that the image was one thing, but a human being was another. He then added, "It's very hard to live up to an image."

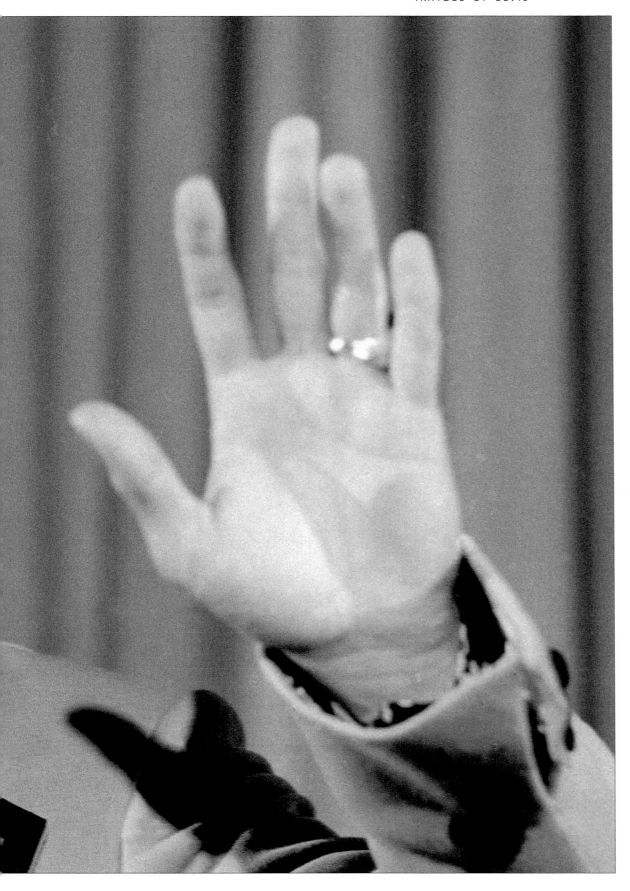

Going through the motions

Left: Despite his bantering with the Press, Elvis was unhappy in his personal life. By now everyone knew that Priscilla had left him – she had finally plucked up the courage to tell him she no longer loved him and that she was seeing someone else. He had introduced some melancholy ballads into his concerts, which he sang with real feeling. This even spilled over into his recording sessions in 1972 – he really needed a hit single but seemed unable to put out anything like the old rock 'n' roll numbers. His last No. 1 had been "Suspicious Minds" in 1969 – he was not to have another No. 1 before his death, although "Burning Love," released in August 1972, went to No. 2.

A Prince from Another Planet

Left: Elvis's father, Vernon, accompanied him to the Madison Square Garden Press conference. When asked how he had reacted to his son's success, he said, "It's kind of hard to say. It happened so fast." All four performances were sold out and the *New York Times* ran a headline, "Like a Prince from Another Planet," the article beneath comparing Elvis to Joe Louis and Joe DiMaggio and calling him "... a champion, the only one in his class."

Jumpsuits galore...

Left: The idea for the famous jumpsuits that Elvis wore in the seventies apparently came from Priscilla, who suggested Elvis should wear them on stage because they would be more comfortable and allow him to move freely. The jumpsuits became increasingly elaborate as time went by.

Opposite: This suit dates from early 1970 and was decorated with tapestry and embroidery.

Putting on the style

Left: Elvis wearing the suit that is also featured on the cover of his album *I Got Lucky*, which was released in 1971. The LP stayed in the *Billboard* album chart for eight weeks, but never got into the top 100. Sometimes he wore this outfit with a woven red belt, as shown here, sometimes he teamed it with a white fringed belt instead.

Back to Vegas

Left: In July 1972 the separation from Priscilla became official, and the following month it was announced that they were seeking a divorce. Elvis's drug intake had increased sharply and news reports were beginning to comment that Elvis sometimes seemed tired or disconnected during concerts. What was more worrying to his close associates was that even in private he was passive and withdrawn – he seemed to have lost his zest for life.

Aloha From Hawaii!

Opposite: In January 1973 the TV special *Aloha From Hawaii* was broadcast to forty countries worldwide, via satellite. The Colonel had also arranged for it to be taped for transmission to a further twenty-eight countries a day later. Elvis was finally pulled out of his lethargy for the occasion, performing songs he had not recorded before and losing weight. He looked slim, fit, and handsome again and the project was a spectacular success.

Left: Elvis at a Press conference in September 1972 in Las Vegas. He announced that he would soon be doing a worldwide concert tour, but nothing came of it. Many suspect that the Colonel stopped it going further as he feared losing control of "his boy."

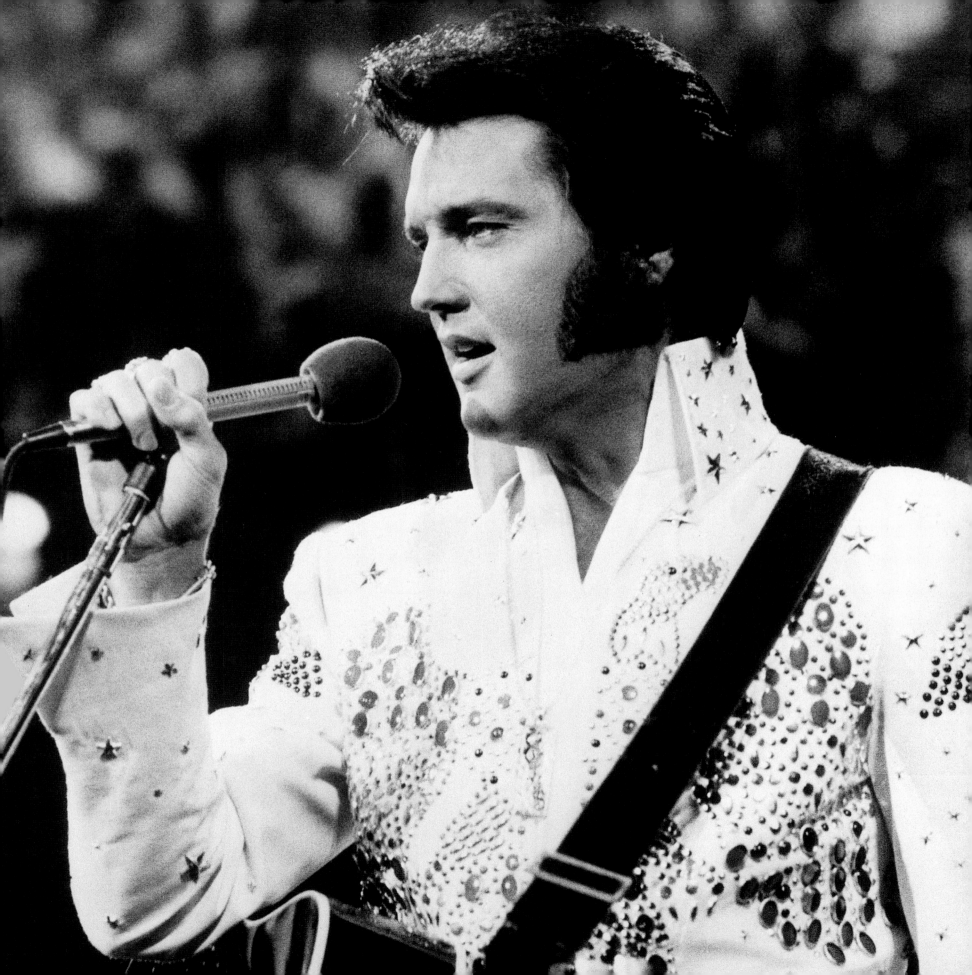

More touring

Opposite: Elvis greets Governor
George C. Wallace in Montgomery,
Alabama, when he performs there at
the Garrett Coliseum. Governor
Wallace and his family were among
an audience of more than 11,000
who came to see the show. The
Governor had returned a day early
from the National Governors'
Conference in Washington to attend
the concert and had proclaimed that
the time that Elvis was in Alabama
should be called Elvis Presley Week.

Right: The new-look Elvis was not to
last for long. He was increasingly
having problems with the amount of
prescription drugs he was taking and
his weight ballooned as a result of his
diet of junk food and lack of exercise.
Those around him tried to help, but
by now he was too used to getting
his own way. Even when he did not
look – or perform – his best, the fans
still loved him and flocked to see him
play, but sometimes he was too ill to
get on stage.

The King is dead...

Right: Elvis was found dead in his bathroom at Graceland on August 16, 1977 by his girlfriend, Ginger Alden. Right from the start confusion surrounded the cause of death because the Shelby County Medical Examiner announced it was due to heart problems before the autopsy was complete. Later the autopsy results confirmed that the drugs had been the true cause – traces of fourteen different medications were found in Elvis's system, with codeine at ten times the recommended level although Elvis had a long-standing mild allergy to it. No official announcement was made, but rumors of drug abuse soon began to circulate.

Elvis has left the building

Opposite: Elvis's flower-covered casket is carried into the mausoleum at Forest Hill Cemetery. Local florists had been flooded with over 3,000 orders for flowers, which had covered the lawn in front of Graceland. It took 100 vehicles four hours to move all the flowers to the cemetery, but Vernon requested that each fan who came to visit the tomb should be given one flower, and within a few hours they were all gone.

Right: The funeral cortège was led by a silver Cadillac and a police motorcycle escort, followed by a white hearse and seventeen white limousines. There were 200 invited guests, but thousands of fans lined the route from Graceland to the cemetery.

Long live the King...

Opposite: After an apparent attempt was made to steal Elvis's body just after the funeral, he and his mother were both moved from Forest Hill and reburied in the Meditation Garden at Graceland in October 1977. Fans still come to pay their respects on each anniversary of his death, and on the evening of August 15 there is a candlelight procession, which often takes many hours to file past his grave. The procession is the culmination of the Tribute Week that Memphis holds each year to honor its most famous resident, with dozens of Elvis-related events to which fans flock from around the globe.

Right: A nine-foot statue of Elvis sculpted by Eric Parks, which was erected on Beale Street in Memphis in 1980. Although some fanatical fans insist their hero has not died but gone undercover in search of a more peaceful lifestyle, most are content to remember him by listening to the music. Many years after his death, his name is still known all around the world and his memory lives on.

CHRONOLOGY

1933

17 Jun   Gladys Love Smith and Vernon Elvis Presley are married

1935

8 Jan   Elvis Aaron Presley is born at his parents' home, 306 Old Saltillo Road; his twin brother, Jesse Garon Presley, is stillborn

1938

25 May   Vernon Presley is sentenced to serve three years at Parchman penal plantation, a Mississippi state penitentiary, and Gladys and Elvis are left to live on welfare

1945

8 Jan   Elvis receives his first guitar for his tenth birthday

3 Oct   At the annual Mississippi–Alabama Fair and Dairy Show, held in Tupelo, Mississippi, Elvis sings "Old Shep" in a live competition and wins second-place prize of five dollars and free admission to the fairground rides

1948

12 Sept   The Presleys move overnight to Memphis, after Vernon is caught trucking for a bootlegger and is fired from his job

1949

20 Sept   The Presleys move into federal-funded accommodation in Memphis and life becomes more stable for nearly three years

1951

3 Jun   Elvis starts work at Precision Tools

1 Jul   Elvis is fired when it is learned that he is under-age

1952

Mar   Elvis plays at the Palm Club on Summer Avenue, Memphis, but the gig goes unnoticed

24 Dec   Elvis sings "Old Shep" and "Cold, Cold Icy Fingers" at his school's Christmas concert to rave reviews

1953

8 Jan   Vernon and Gladys pay $50 for a 1942 Lincoln Zephyr coupé, as an 18th-birthday present for Elvis

26 May   After hitchhiking to Meridian, Mississippi, Elvis sings at the First Jimmie Rodgers Memorial Talent Show at the Lamar Hotel and wins

the second-place guitar prize with a country version of "I'm Left, You're Right, She's Gone" and a rock version of "Baby, Let's Play House"

3 Jun   Elvis graduates from Class 202 at Humes High School

Summer   Elvis records "My Happiness" and "That's When Your Heartache Begins" at Sam Phillips's Memphis Recording Service; he takes the original pressing and no copies are made

1954

4 Jan   Elvis records "I'll Never Stand In Your Way" and "Casual Love Affair" at Sam Phillips's Memphis Recording Service; again, he takes the original pressing and no copies are made

Jan   Dixie Locke becomes Elvis's first serious girlfriend

May   Sam Phillips asks Elvis to sing "Without You," but is not impressed; however, he calls guitarist Scotty Moore and bass player Bill Black, and asks them to work with Elvis; the three rehearse for weeks at Phillips's Sun Studios

5–6 Jul   Elvis, Scotty Moore and Bill Black record "That's All Right, Mama" and "Blue Moon of Kentucky" at Sun Studios

7 Jul   Sam Phillips sends out DJ demos of the first record, and Dewey Phillips plays "That's All Right, Mama" on WHBQ 14 times in a row; later that evening, Elvis is interviewed on-air

11 Jul   Elvis, Scotty Moore and Bill Black, along with Johnny Bernero on drums, record "Mystery Train" at Sun Studios

12 Jul   Elvis and his parents sign a one-year contract with Scotty Moore

19 Jul   Official release of the first record "That's All Right, Mama"/"Blue Moon Of Kentucky," which quickly sells 20,000 copies

28 Jul   The first published interview with Elvis appears in "The Front Row" in the *Press-Scimitar*

30 Jul   Elvis appears in his first major concert, at the Overton Park Shell

7 Aug   *Billboard* reviews "That's All Right, Mama," giving it a good write-up

Aug–Oct   Elvis and the Blue Moon Boys perform several times in Texas and at the Eagle's Nest, Memphis whenever they can

25 Sept   Elvis and the Blue Moon Boys

appear at Nashville's Grand Ole Opry, but do not go down well; Elvis never performed there again

25 Sept   Release of "Good Rockin' Tonight"/"I Don't Care If The Sun Don't Shine"

Oct   Promoter Oscar "The Baron" Davis brings Elvis to the attention of his boss, Colonel Tom Parker; the Colonel comes to see him perform and they meet for the first time, at Taylor's restaurant, along with Scotty, Bill Black, the Baron and Bob Neal

16 Oct   Elvis and the Blue Moon Boys appear on a radio show, the *Louisiana Hayride*, which went out across the southern US on KWKH from Shreveport's Municipal Auditorium; he is an instant success

23 Oct   Elvis and the Blue Moon Boys perform again at the Louisiana Hayride

6 Nov   Elvis and the Blue Moon Boys perform at the Louisiana Hayride and afterwards sign a one-year contract to appear every Saturday

Dec   Elvis and the Blue Moon Boys appear each week on the Louisiana Hayride show

10 Dec   Elvis records "Milkcow Blues Boogie" at Sun Records

18 Dec   "I'm Left, You're Right, She's Gone" and a version of "My Baby's Gone" are recorded at Sun Studios

1955

1 Jan   The OK Group hires Elvis for one-night performances on the radio at $300 a time

8 Jan   "Milkcow Blues Boogie"/"You're A Heartbreaker" is released, but does not chart

16 Jan   Elvis and the band appear at a concert in Booneville, Mississippi, part of which is broadcast by WBIP. Further concerts follow at Eagle's Nest, Houston and Lake Pontchartrain, New Orleans

Feb   Colonel Parker attempts to get RCA interested in Elvis, but although Steve Sholes, RCA's man in Nashville, is interested, the record company is not

Feb   Elvis and the band continue to appear at the Louisiana Hayride on Saturday nights and also play concerts in Carlsbad, New Mexico, Albuquerque, Texas, Louisiana, Arkansas, and Cleveland

5 Mar   Elvis makes his TV debut when the Louisiana Hayride is broadcast regionally

Mar   Elvis and the boys appear in concerts in Tennessee, Louisiana, Arkansas, Mississippi and Missouri

19 Mar   Elvis appears live on the *Grand Prize Saturday Night Jamboree*, broadcast from Eagle's Hall in Houston, Texas, by KPRC-TV; he also records "I Got A Woman" at the same venue

1 Apr   "Baby, Let's Play House"/"I'm Left, You're Right, She's Gone" is released

1 May   Elvis performs in New Orleans and then begins a three-week tour through Chattanooga with Hank Snow's All-Star Jamboree

25 May   Elvis performs at the Jimmie Rodgers Memorial Day Celebration in Meridian, Mississippi

31 May   An afternoon concert in Midland, Texas is followed by a live radio appearance on *The Roy Orbison Show* in Odessa

26 Jun   After a concert in Biloxi, Mississippi, Elvis meets June Juanico, whom he dates on and off for a year

Jul   "Baby, Let's Play House" makes it into the *Billboard* Top Ten

6 Aug   Release of "I Forgot To Remember To Forget"/"Mystery Train", which later goes into the *Billboard* country chart for 40 weeks

15 Aug   Elvis signs a contract giving Colonel Parker the right to manage his career, although he is still bound to Bob Neal for a year

   "Mystery Train" enters the *Billboard* country chart, staying there for 30 weeks

8 Sept   Elvis signs a new contract with the Louisiana Hayride for a further year from 8 November; his payment increases from $18 a night to $200

Oct   Atlantic Records bids $25,000 for Elvis to sign with them, but is turned down

10 Nov   Elvis secures the recording rights to "Heartbreak Hotel" from Mae Axton

20 Nov   Sun Records' contract with Elvis is bought for $25,000 by RCA Victor, while Hill and Range Music buys Sam Phillips's Hi-Lo music publishing company for $15,000

22 Nov   Elvis signs a contract making Colonel Parker his exclusive representative

1956

5 Jan Colonel Parker does a deal with Hill and Range Music, establishing a 50/50 partnership for five years with the newly created Presley Music Inc to publish the songs Elvis records

9 Jan Elvis rehearses "Heartbreak Hotel" before recording it for RCA the following day, along with "I Got A Woman"; the next day, he records "I Was The One" and "I'm Counting On You"

17 Jan Release of "Heartbreak Hotel"/"I Was The One"

28 Jan Elvis appears on Milton Berle's *Stage Show* on CBS TV

30/31 Jan "Blue Suede Shoes" is recorded during a two-day studio session

15 Feb "I Forgot To Remember To Forget"/"Mystery Train" both reach No. 1 on the *Billboard* country chart

22 Feb "Heartbreak Hotel" enters the *Billboard* Top 100 at No. 68 and the Country's Best Sellers in Stores chart at No. 9

29 Feb "I Was The One" enters the *Billboard* Top 100 at No. 84

1 Mar RCA is overwhelmed with 362,000 advance orders for the first LP, "Elvis Presley"

13 Mar Release of the LP, "Elvis Presley," which goes on to become the first in history to sell a million copies

15 Mar Colonel Parker becomes the sole official manager of Elvis

28 Mar "Blue Suede Shoes" enters the *Billboard* Top 100 chart at No. 88

1 Apr Elvis does a screen-test for Hal Wallis of Paramount Pictures

Apr "Heartbreak Hotel" is No. 1 on the *Billboard* pop chart

6 Apr Paramount Pictures signs Elvis to a seven-year, three-movie contract

May Release of "I Want You, I Need You, I Love You," which stays in the *Billboard* Top 100 for 24 weeks and reaches No. 3, also getting to No. 10 on the R&B chart and No. 1 for one week on the country chart; the flipside was "My Baby Left Me"

11 Apr *Variety* claims that "Heartbreak Hotel" has become the first Presley record to sell a million copies

23 Apr Elvis begins a four-week engagement at the New Frontier Hotel, Las Vegas, but the audience does not respond well to him and he only stays for two weeks

Jun RCA releases the EP "Elvis Presley," which goes on to stay in the *Billboard* Top 100 for 12 weeks, reaching No. 24

1 Jul Elvis appears on *The Steve Allen Show*, singing "Hound Dog"

20 Aug Elvis begins filming *Love Me Tender* in Hollywood

5 Sept "Don't Be Cruel"/"Hound Dog" reaches No. 1 on the *Billboard* Top 100

9 Sept *The Ed Sullivan Show* gets the highest ratings in television history when Elvis appears

19 Sept "Blue Moon" enters the *Billboard* Top 100 at No. 87

Sept Release of "Tryin' To Get To You"/"I Love You Because," "Blue Suede Shoes"/"Tutti Frutti" and "One-Sided Love Affair"/"Money Honey," none of which charts

Oct Elvis receives his draft questionnaire

3 Oct "I Don't Care If The Sun Don't Shine" enters the *Billboard* Top 100 at No. 77

8 Oct *Time* reveals that RCA has advance orders of one million for the single "Love Me Tender" – an all-time high

10 Oct "Love Me Tender"/"Any Way You Want Me" enters the *Billboard* Top 100 at No. 9

19 Oct The LP "Elvis" is released

24 Oct Elvis earns a gold record for "Love Me Tender," his fifth of the year

Nov The LPs "Elvis Vol 1" and "Elvis Vol 2" are released

7 Nov "Love Me Tender" enters the *Billboard* Top 100 at No. 84, the LP "Elvis" enters the Best Selling Packaged Records – Popular Albums at No. 7, and "Love Me Tender" reaches No. 1 on the Top 100

15 Nov The movie *Love Me Tender* opens

Dec Release of the LP "Love Me Tender"

15 Dec Elvis appears at the Louisiana Hayride for the last time

Dec "Heartbreak Hotel" is the *Billboard* No. 1 single for 1956

1957

6 Jan Elvis appears for the final time on *The Ed Sullivan Show*

Jan The Army announces that Elvis is classed 1-A for draft

21 Jan Start of the filming of *Loving You*

Jan Release of "Too Much"/"Playing For Keeps," which stays in the *Billboard* Top 100 for 17 weeks, at No. 2 for four of them

7 Mar Elvis pays $102,500 for Graceland, far outbidding an offer of $35,000 from the YMCA

10 Apr "All Shook Up" reaches No. 1 on the *Billboard* Top 100 and stays there for eight weeks

13 May Start of shooting on *Jailhouse Rock*

June "Teddy Bear"/"Loving You" is the first Elvis single to be distributed in the UK, and sells over a million copies

9 Jul Premiere of *Loving You* at the Strand Theater in Memphis

27 Jul "Teddy Bear"/"Loving You" hits No. 1 on the *Billboard* Top 100 and stays there for 17 weeks, it is also at No. 1 for one week on both the R&B and the country charts

Sept The single "Jailhouse Rock"/"Treat Me Nice" is released in the UK and becomes the first Elvis record to enter the charts at No. 1 in England; it has already been released in the US and goes on to sell over three million copies in 12 months

28 Sept The LP "Elvis Presley" reaches No. 1 on the *Billboard* extended-play album chart staying for six weeks

8 Nov *Jailhouse Rock* opens across the country and goes on to make a profit within three weeks

19 Dec Elvis receives his draft notice

1958

Jan Release of "I Beg Of You," which stays in the *Billboard* Top 100 for 12 weeks

5 Mar Filming starts on *King Creole*

24 Mar Elvis is inducted into the Army and is sent to Fort Chaffee, Arkansas

28 Mar Elvis is sent to Fort Hood with his battalion for basic training

1 Jul *King Creole* is released to good reviews

5 Aug Gladys is taken into the hospital and Elvis is granted compassionate leave to visit her

11 Aug Elvis receives his first RIAA Gold Disk Award for "Hard-Headed Woman"

14 Aug Gladys dies of a heart attack in the hospital

16 Aug Gladys's funeral is held in Memphis and she is buried at Forest Hill Cemetery

24 Aug As his unit is soon being sent to Germany, Elvis returns to basic training

19 Sept With his Army unit, Elvis travels from Fort Hood to Brooklyn, New York

22 Sept Elvis and his unit leave on the USS *General Randall* for Bremerhaven, Germany, where they disembark to transfer to Friedberg

10 Oct The entourage moves into a rented house, and Elvis moves off base to join them

27 Nov Elvis is promoted to private first class

1959

1 Jun Elvis is promoted to specialist fourth class

3–9 Jun Elvis gets tonsillitis and is sent to Frankfurt Military Hospital

Nov Priscilla Beaulieu is introduced to Elvis at a party

Nov Vernon meets Dee Stanley, an American in Germany with her husband and family

25 Dec Elvis takes Priscilla to local festivities and meets her parents

1960

20 Jan Elvis is promoted to sergeant

17 Feb The RIAA finally certifies the LP "Elvis" a Gold Disk – although it has already sold more than three million copies

2 Mar Elvis leaves Germany from Wiesbaden airport and arrives the following day at McGuire Air Force Base at Fort Dix

3 Apr Release of the LP "Elvis Is Back," which goes on to stay in the *Billboard* chart for 56 weeks

3 Apr "It's Now Or Never"/"A Mess Of Blues" is recorded, going on to achieve sales of well over 23 million copies

4 Apr "Are You Lonesome Tonight?" is recorded and makes the largest chart leap so far, entering the *Billboard* Hot 100 at No. 35 but jumping to No. 2 within 7 days

1 May Elvis and his entourage arrive at the Beverly Wilshire to begin filming on *GI Blues* for Paramount

12 May *The Frank Sinatra – Timex Special*, featuring Elvis and recorded at the Fontainbleau Hotel in Miami Beach, is broadcast on ABC TV

3 Jul Vernon marries Dee Stanley, but Elvis refuses to attend the wedding

20 Jul Vernon brings Dee and her three sons to Graceland, but they soon move to a house on Dolan Avenue

15 Aug Filming begins on *Flaming Star*

11 Nov Filming begins on *Wild in the Country* for Twentieth Century Fox

23 Nov National release of *GI Blues*, which reaches No. 2 in *Variety*'s list of top-grossing movies

1961

18 Jan Filming finishes on *Wild in the Country*

14 Mar Elvis flies to California with his entourage to begin filming on *Blue Hawaii* for Paramount and flies to Hawaii 10 days later

15 Jun *Wild in the Country* is premiered, then released nationwide

11 Jul Filming begins on *Follow That Dream* for United Artists

5–14 Nov Elvis is coached for the boxing scenes in *Kid Galahad* by former junior welterweight champion Mush Callahan

Nov Filming begins on *Kid Galahad*

21 Nov *Blue Hawaii* is released nationally and, by the end of the year, has grossed $4.7 million

1962

7 Apr Elvis flies to Hawaii to begin filming on *Girls! Girls! Girls!* for Paramount

23 May National release of *Follow That Dream*

June After negotiations with her stepfather, Priscilla Beaulieu arrives in Los Angeles from Germany to spend some time with Elvis

27 Aug Filming begins on *It Happened at the World's Fair* for MGM

29 Aug National release of *Kid Galahad*, which goes on to gross $1.7 million by the end of the year

Oct Release of "Return To Sender"/"Where Do You Come From?", which reaches No. 2 on the *Billboard* Hot 100, No. 5 on the R&B chart and was No. 1 for three weeks in the UK

Nov Elvis returns to Graceland for three weeks

21 Nov National release of *Girls! Girls! Girls!*, which goes on to gross $2.6 million by the end of the year

Dec Priscilla's parents are persuaded to let her come to America to spend Christmas with Elvis at Graceland

1963

Jan Priscilla returns to Germany, but Elvis asks her stepfather if she can move to America and finish her education in Memphis

28 Jan Filming begins on *Fun in Acapulco*

Mar Priscilla moves into Graceland and is enrolled at the Immaculate Conception High School

3 Apr Premiere of *It Happened at the World's Fair* in Los Angeles

10 Apr Nationwide opening of *It Happened at the World's Fair*, which goes on to gross $2.25 million by the end of the year

29 May Priscilla graduates from the Immaculate Conception High School

15 Jul Filming begins on *Viva Las Vegas*

5 Oct Filming begins on *Kissin' Cousins*

21 Oct Filming finishes on *Kissin' Cousins*

27 Nov National release of *Fun in Acapulco*, which goes on to gross over $1.5 million by the end of the year

1964

9 Mar Filming begins on *Roustabout*

Apr *Kissin' Cousins* opens nationally

20 Apr Premiere of *Viva Las Vegas* in New York; filming finishes on *Roustabout*

17 Jun National release of *Viva Las Vegas*, which goes on to gross over $4.5 million by the end of the year

22 Jun Filming begins on *Girl Happy*

6 Oct Filming begins on *Tickle Me*

11 Nov National release of *Roustabout*, which goes on to gross $3 million by the end of the year

1965

8 Jan Elvis celebrates his 30th birthday at Graceland

15 Mar Filming begins on *Harum Scarum*

Apr Elvis starts to visit the Self-Realization Fellowship Center and later meets its president, Sri Daya Mata

14 Apr National release of *Girl Happy*, which goes on to gross $3.1 million by the end of the year

25 May Filming begins on *Frankie and Johnny* for United Artists

28 May Premiere of *Tickle Me* in Atlanta

7 Aug Filming begins on *Paradise, Hawaiian Style*

27 Aug The Beatles and Brian Epstein meet Elvis at his Bel Air home

24 Nov Premiere of *Harum Scarum*

Dec Elvis moves from Perugia Way, Bel Air, to Rocca Place in Stone Canyon

1966

20 Feb Filming begins on *Spinout*

31 Mar Premiere of *Frankie and Johnny* in Baton Rouge, Louisiana

6 Apr Filming finishes on *Spinout*

11 Jun Filming begins on *Double Trouble*

6 Jul Nationwide release of *Paradise, Hawaiian Style*, which goes on to gross over $2.5 million by the end of the year

5 Sept Filming finishes on *Double Trouble*

12 Sept Filming begins on *Easy Come, Easy Go* for Paramount

1 Nov The RIAA certifies the LP "Elvis Presley" as a Platinum Disk after it has sold a million copies

23 Nov Nationwide release of *Spinout*

Dec Both her parents and the Colonel insist that it is time Elvis marries Priscilla or that she moves out of Graceland so, just before Christmas, he finally proposes

1967

9 Feb Elvis buys the Circle G Ranch in Walls, Mississippi

Mar Filming begins on *Clambake*

22 Mar Opening of *Easy Come, Easy Go*

5 Apr Nationwide release of *Double Trouble*, which soon grosses $1.6 million

1 May Elvis marries Priscilla Beaulieu at the Aladdin Hotel, Las Vegas, in a private ceremony

2/6 May Elvis and Priscilla honeymoon in Palm Springs, California, and then go on to the Circle G Ranch, accompanied by some of the Memphis Mafia

7 May Elvis and Priscilla move to a new home in Hillcrest Road, Beverly Hills

29 May A second wedding ceremony is held at Graceland, as many people were excluded from the first

12 Jun Filming begins on *Speedway*

18 Oct Filming begins on *Stay Away, Joe*

22 Nov Release of *Clambake*

8 Dec TV premiere of *Tickle Me* on CBS TV's *Friday Night at the Movies*

Dec Elvis receives a Grammy Award for Best Sacred Performance for "How Great Thou Art"

1968

1 Feb Lisa Marie Presley is born at the Baptist Memorial Hospital

Feb Release of "Elvis" Gold Records, Vol 4

8 Mar National distribution of *Stay Away, Joe*

27/30 Jun Elvis tapes a TV special for NBC TV, and is persuaded to appear in black leather and go back to his musical roots

Jul Filming begins on *Live a Little, Love a Little*

22 Jul Work commences on *Charro!*

23 Oct Release of *Live a Little, Love a Little*

28 Oct Filming begins on *The Trouble with Girls* for MGM

3 Dec The comeback TV special *Elvis* is broadcast on NBC TV and is the highest-rated program that week

1969

10 Mar Filming begins on *Change of Habit*

13 Mar National release of *Charro!*

2 May Filming of *Change of Habit* is completed

May Elvis decides that he no longer wants to act in movies, but would like to return to singing

21 May The Circle G Ranch is sold and the horses moved to Graceland

15 Jun "In the Ghetto" is certified gold

31 Jul At the International Hotel, Las Vegas, Elvis appears live in concert for the first time in eight years

Sept "Suspicious Minds"/"You'll Think Of Me" is released and goes into the *Billboard* Top 100 for 15 weeks, reaching No. 1 in November

22 Aug The *Elvis* TV comeback special is broadcast again

3 Sept National release of the movie *The Trouble with Girls*

10 Nov National release of *Change of Habit*

12 Dec The LP "From Memphis to Vegas/From Vegas to Memphis" is certified gold by the RIAA

1970

21 Jan "Don't Cry Daddy" sells a million copies and is certified gold by the RIAA

26 Jan A new season of 57 concerts begins at the International Hotel, Las Vegas

1 Mar Elvis flies back to Memphis to rest; after checking into the Baptist Memorial Hospital, he is informed that he has glaucoma in his left eye

10 Aug The first concert in a new season at the International Hotel, Las Vegas

9 Sept Elvis gives a concert at the Veterans Memorial Coliseum in Phoenix, Arizona, and goes on to appear in St Louis, Detroit, Miami Beach, Tampa and Mobile over the next few days

11 Nov The premiere of *Elvis – That's The Way It Is*

21 Dec During a meeting with President Nixon, Elvis is given a Narcotics Bureau badge

1971

Jan/Feb A season of 57 concerts at the International Hotel, Las Vegas

20 Jul Elvis plays the first of 28 concerts at the Sahara Tahoe Hotel in Stateline, Nevada followed by another season of 57 shows at the Hilton Hotel in Las Vegas

Nov Elvis performs concerts in Minneapolis, Cleveland, Louisville, Philadelphia, Baltimore, Boston, Cincinnati, Houston, Dallas, Tuscaloosa, Kansas City, and Salt Lake City

30 Dec Elvis tells his companions that Priscilla has left him

1972

26 Jan The first of a new season of 57 concerts at the Las Vegas Hilton

Apr A series of concerts are played at Buffalo in New York, Detroit, Dayton, Knoxville, Hampton Roads in Virginia, Richmond, Roanoke, Indianapolis, Charlotte, Greensboro, Macon, Jacksonville, Little Rock, San Antonio, and Albuquerque; many of them are filmed for the documentary *Elvis on Tour*

6 Jun	Elvis plays the opening concert of four at Madison Square Garden in New York followed by a short tour
6 Jul	Elvis meets Linda Thompson, a former beauty queen
26 Jul	Elvis and Priscilla are legally separated
4 Aug	The opening concert of 63 at the Las Vegas Hilton
18 Aug	Elvis files for divorce from Priscilla
Sept	Linda Thompson moves into Graceland
1 Nov	Release of *Elvis on Tour*, which grosses nearly half a million dollars in one week
Nov	A series of concerts are played in Lubbock, Tucson, El Paso, Oakland, San Bernadino, Long Beach, and Honolulu
Dec	A Grammy for Best Inspirational Performance is awarded for the LP "He Touched Me"

1973

14 Jan	Elvis: *Aloha From Hawaii* is broadcast to 40 countries worldwide
15 Jan	A second broadcast of *Elvis: Aloha From Hawaii* is seen in 28 European countries
26 Jan	Elvis performs the opening concert of 54 at the Las Vegas Hilton
Apr	Concerts are played in Phoenix, Anaheim, Fresno, San Diego, Portland, Spokane, Seattle, and, Denver
4 May	Elvis is due to play 25 concerts at the Sahara Tahoe Hotel in Stateline, Nevada, but several concerts are canceled due to illness, as years of prescription drug abuse begin to take their toll
18 May	Ill and exhausted, Elvis returns to Memphis
Jun	Concerts are played in Mobile, Atlanta, Uniondale, Nassau, Pittsburgh, Cincinnati, St. Louis, Nashville, and Oklahoma City. After returning to Memphis in July, Elvis begins a series of recording sessions
6 Aug	The first concert in a planned series of 59 at the Las Vegas Hilton, although Elvis misses two due to illness
Aug	After a major argument the partnership of Colonel Parker and Elvis breaks up, but is soon reinstated
9 Oct	The divorce of Elvis and Priscilla is finalized in Santa Monica
Oct	Elvis is hospitalized for two weeks after an extreme drug reaction and is put through a drug withdrawal program
10/16 Dec	Elvis records several songs in a session at Stax Studios in Memphis

1974

Jan	Colonel Parker and Elvis form Boxcar Enterprises to handle the merchandizing of Elvis-related products not connected to movies or records; Boxcar Records is also created
26 Jan	The first concert in a series of 29 at the Las Vegas Hilton ending February 9
Mar	*Silver Screen* features Elvis on its cover and an article speculates that he will marry Linda Thompson
Mar	Concerts are played in Tulsa, Houston, Monroe in Louisiana, Auburn in Alabama, Montgomery, Charlotte, Roanoke, Hampton Roads, Richmond, Greensboro, Murfreesboro in Tennessee, Knoxville, and Memphis
Mar	Dr George Nichopoulos (Dr Nick) attends Elvis full time during the tour so he can monitor his drug intake
May	Concerts are played in San Bernadino, Los Angeles, and Fresno followed by 22 dates at the Sahara Tahoe Hotel in Stateline, Nevada
Jun	A 21-day tour begins
Oct	Concerts are played in St. Paul in Minnesota, Dayton, Indianapolis, Wichita, San Antonio, and Abilene followed by eight concerts at the Sahara Tahoe Hotel in Stateline, Nevada
Dec	Elvis recuperates from a strenuous year at Graceland and an article in *Celebrity* comments on his poor health

1975

29 Jan	Elvis is rushed to the hospital at midnight with severe stomach pains, and is admitted to get his drug use back under control
5 Feb	Elvis's father Vernon has a heart attack and is admitted to the same hospital
10/13 Mar	Elvis records at RCA's Hollywood studios
18 Mar	The first of a scheduled 29 shows at the Las Vegas Hilton
Apr–Jul	Concerts are scheduled all across the United States
18 Aug	Although he is due to perform a series of concerts at the Las Vegas Hilton, most of them are canceled due to Elvis's poor health
21 Aug	Elvis is admitted to the hospital for two weeks and attempts are made to solve some of his medical problems
28 Nov	Elvis flies to Las Vegas to rehearse for 17 shows at the Las Vegas Hilton, and Linda Thompson returns briefly to support him

31 Dec	A New Year's Eve concert in Pontiac, Michigan, breaks concert receipt records

1976

22 Jan	A new agreement giving the Colonel 50/50 partnership on live dates comes into effect
Apr/Jun	Concerts are played in Kansas City, Omaha, Denver, San Diego, Long Beach, Seattle, 15 shows at the Sahara Tahoe Hotel in Stateline, Nevada, Bloomington, Ames in Iowa, Oklahoma City, Odessa in Texas, Lubbock, Tucson, El Paso, Fort Worth, Atlanta, Omaha, Buffalo, Rhode Island, Largo in Maryland, Philadelphia, Richmond, and Greensboro
Jul/Aug	Concerts are performed at Shreveport, Baton Rouge, Fort Worth, Tulsa, Memphis, Louisville, Charleston, Syracuse, Rochester, Hartford, Springfield, New Haven, Hampton Roads, Roanoke, San Antonio, Houston, Mobile, Tuscaloosa, and Macon
Sept/Oct	Elvis performs concerts in Jacksonville, Florida, Alabama, Arkansas, Duluth, Minneapolis, Sioux Falls, Madison, South Bend, Kalamazoo, Champaign, Cleveland, Evansville, Fort Wayne, Dayton, and Carbondale, Illinois
29 Oct	Another recording session is arranged at Graceland, but Elvis is not well enough to do much work
19 Nov	Elvis meets Ginger Alden, a former beauty queen
Nov	Elvis performs a series of concerts in Nevada, Oregon, and California, and Ginger Alden is invited to join him; Linda Thompson finally leaves for good
2 Dec	A new season of 15 concerts begins at the Las Vegas Hilton; the last is on December 12, and Elvis does not miss any performances
9 Dec	Vernon is admitted to the hospital with a suspected heart attack
27 Dec	The first of five concerts is performed in Wichita, Kansas; the others are in Texas, Alabama, Georgia, and Pennsylvania

1977

26 Jan	Elvis proposes to Ginger and gives her a diamond ring
Feb–Mar	A series of 17 concerts are played in across America
3 Mar	Elvis takes Ginger and her family on a two-week vacation to Hawaii
Apr	A series of concerts is booked but Elvis collapses during the tour, and is taken back to Memphis and admitted to the Baptist Memorial Hospital

5 Apr	Elvis leaves the hospital and spends some time recuperating at Graceland
May/Jun	A series of 23 concerts is performed across 18 states with only 16 days' rest
Jul	Release of "Way Down"/"Pledging My Love," which goes into the *Billboard* country chart for 17 weeks, reaching No. 1 in August; it also spends 21 weeks in the Top 100 chart, reaching No. 18, and reaches No. 14 on the easy listening chart; in the UK it becomes Elvis's 17th No. 1 record
Jul/Aug	Lisa Marie arrives at Graceland for a two-week visit
16 Aug	Elvis is found dead in his bathroom at Graceland by Ginger Alden; the cause of death is announced as a heart attack, but the later autopsy rules that he died from a drug overdose
17 Aug	With his body lying in state at Graceland, thousands of fans congregate outside, waiting to file past the coffin and get one last glimpse of Elvis
18 Aug	Elvis's funeral is held at Graceland, and he is laid to rest next to his mother at Forest Hill Cemetery
27 Oct	The bodies of Elvis and his mother are removed from Forest Hill Cemetery and re-interred at Graceland in the Meditation Garden

Picture Credits

The photographs in this book are reproduced by kind permission of Getty Images and Corbis:

Getty Images

8, 14, 18, 19, 20, 21, 22, 24 (and 8), 25, 42, 44, 45, 48, 49, 50, 51, 52, 53, 54, 55, 57, 69, 93, 126, 130, 131, 142, 152, 161, 165, 177, 186, 188

Corbis

6 John Springer Collection/Corbis; 12 John Springer Collection/Corbis; 15 Bettman/Corbis; 16 Corbis; 17 Bettman/Corbis; 26 Bettman/Corbis; 28 John Springer Collection/Corbis; 29 Bettman/Corbis; 30 Bettman/Corbis; 31 Bettman/Corbis; 32 Bettman/Corbis; 33 Bettman/Corbis; 34 (and 3) Bettman/Corbis; 36 Bettman/Corbis; 37 Bettman/Corbis; 38 Bettman/Corbis; 39 John Springer Collection/Corbis; 40 Bettman/Corbis; 41 Corbis; 46 Bettman/Corbis; 56 Bettman/Corbis; 58 Bettman/Corbis; 59 Bettman/Corbis; 60 Corbis; 61 Bettman/Corbis; 62 Bettman/Corbis; 64 John Springer Collection/Corbis; 65 Bettman/Corbis; 66 Bettman/Corbis; 67 John Springer Collection/Corbis; 68 (and 1) John Springer Collection/Corbis; 71 Bettman/Corbis; 72 Bettman/Corbis; 74 Bettman/Corbis; 75 Bettman/Corbis; 76 Bettman/Corbis; 78 Corbis; 79 Bettman/Corbis; 80 John Springer Collection/Corbis; 81 Bettman/Corbis; 82 Corbis; 83 Bettman/Corbis; 84 Bettman/Corbis; 85 Bettman/Corbis; 86 Bettman/Corbis; 88 Bettman/Corbis; 89 Bettman/Corbis; 90 Bettman/Corbis; 91 Bettman/Corbis; 92 Bettman/Corbis; 94 Bettman/Corbis; 97 Bettman/Corbis; 98 Bettman/ Corbis; 100 Corbis; 101 Bettman/Corbis; 102 Bettman/Corbis; 103 Bettman/Corbis; 104 Bettman/Corbis; 105 Bettman/Corbis; 106 Corbis; 107 Bettman/Corbis; 108 Bettman/Corbis; 109 Bettman/Corbis; 110 Bettman/Corbis; 111 Bettman/Corbis; 112 Bettman/Corbis; 114 Bettman/Corbis; 116 (and 2) John Springer Collection/Corbis; 117 Bettman/Corbis; 118 Bettman/Corbis; 119 Bettman/Corbis; 120 Bettman/Corbis; 121 Bettman/Corbis; 122 Bettman/Corbis; 123 Bettman/Corbis; 124 Bettman/Corbis; 128 Seattle Post-Intelligencer Collection/Corbis; 129 Bettman/Corbis; 132 (and 4) Bettman/Corbis; 134 Bettman/Corbis; 136 Bettman/Corbis; 137 Bettman/Corbis; 138 Bettman/Corbis; 140 Bettman/Corbis; 141 Bettman/Corbis; 144 Bettman/Corbis; 146 Bettman/Corbis; 147 John Springer Collection/Corbis 148 Bettman/Corbis; 150 (and 9) Bettman/Corbis; 151 Bettman/Corbis; 154 Bettman/Corbis; 155 Bettman/Corbis; 157 Bettman/Corbis; 158 Bettman/Corbis; 159 Bettman/Corbis; 160 Bettman/Corbis; 162 Bettman/Corbis; 166 Frank Carroll/ Sygma/Corbis; 167 Frank Carroll/Sygma/Corbis; 168 Frank Carroll/ Sygma/Corbis; 169 (and 10) Frank Carroll/ Sygma/Corbis; 170 Frank Carroll/ Sygma/Corbis; 171 Frank Carroll/ Sygma/Corbis; 172 Frank Carroll/ Sygma/Corbis; 173 Frank Carroll/ Sygma/Corbis; 174 Frank Carroll/ Sygma/Corbis; 175 Bettman/Corbis; 176 Bettman/Corbis; 179 Bettman/Corbis; 180 Frank Carroll/ Sygma; 181 Frank Carroll/ Sygma; 182 Frank Carroll/ Sygma; 183 Frank Carroll/ Sygma; 184 Frank Carroll/ Sygma; 185 Frank Carroll/ Sygma; 187 Corbis; 189 Lynn Goldsmith/Corbis; 190 Bettman/Corbis; 191 Frank Carroll/ Sygma; 192 Frank Carroll/ Sygma; 193 Frank Carroll/ Sygma; 194 Frank Carroll/ Sygma; 195 Frank Carroll/ Sygma; 196 Jeff Albertson/Corbis; 197 Jeff Albertson/Corbis; 198 Bettman/Corbis; 200 Jeff Albertson/Corbis; 202 Bettman/Corbis; 203 Bettman/Corbis; 204 Sam Emerson/ Sygma; 206 (and11) Sam Emerson/ Sygma; 208 Bettman/Corbis; 209Bettman/Corbis; 210 Bettman/Corbis; 211 Sam Emerson/Sygma; 212 Bettman/Corbis; 214 Bettman/Corbis; 215 Bettman/Corbis; 216 Henry Diltz/Corbis; 217 Franz-Marc Frei/Corbis

Cover images courtesy of Corbis